DELIRIUM VITAE

DAVID LeBRUN

DELIRIUM VITAE

DAVID LeBRUN

TORTOISE BOOKS

CHICAGO

FIRST EDITION, June, 2025

Copyright © 2025 by David LeBrun

All rights reserved under International and Pan-American Copyright Convention

Published in the United States and Canada by Tortoise Books

www.tortoisebooks.com

ISBN-13: 978- 1965199022

This book is a work of memoir, and is drawn from the author's experience, notes, recordings, and recollections. Dialogue is approximate and appears in quotation marks for the benefit of the reader. For readability, some timelines have been altered, and some characters were merged. To protect privacy, names and identifying details have been changed.

Front Cover Notepad by Talleres Estrella, Mexico. Front Cover Design by David LeBrun. Copyright © 2025 by Tortoise Books

Tortoise Books Logo Copyright ©2025 by Tortoise Books. Original artwork by Rachele O'Hare

"He was free, but too infinitely free; not striding upon the earth but floating above it. He felt the lack in him of that weight of human relations that trammels a man's progress; tears, farewells, reproaches, joys— all those things that a man caresses or rips apart each time he sketches a gesture; those thousand ties that bind him to others and lend density to his being."

– Antoine de Saint-Exupéry

CHAPTER ONE

I dropped to the dirt. The Arizona sun burned red on my eyelids. The right side of my face went numb, and my skull ballooned until my mind burst into a thousand thoughts—all floating toward death.

"Hey, what happened to you?"

•

In 2001, I was twenty-four and on my seventeenth job since dropping out of university. I'd been a security guard, house painter, pool boy, smelter labourer, sheet metal labourer, tree planter, plastic products inspector. I'd even worked in a button warehouse. I'd quit every job I'd had because they'd all shoved me in a corner and stolen the time I needed to become a writer.

My father had wanted me to stay in school and find a good job—to live a practical, ordinary life. If he'd lived long enough to hear me say I wanted to be a writer, he would have died of laughter. When he was younger, he played piano. But life in a gold mine had extracted from him any urge to create. He'd worked at the mine for twenty years, but I'd never heard him talk about it. And before I was a teenager, our upright piano had been cut to pieces, lugged out of the basement, and dumped in a landfill like an old doghouse. It was at seventeen, after watching his cancer devour him, that I knew I wanted nothing in my life to be ordinary.

Now I was working and living on a broccoli farm in Southern Ontario with sixteen migrant Mexican workers. One day Bard, the farmer, called me into the house. I thought he'd caught me getting high, which I'd been doing every morning, lunch break, and evening for four months. I slowly dragged my work boots across the lot, convinced that for the first time in my life, I was getting fired.

When Bard opened the door, towering over me like a balding grizzly bear with glasses, he said, "Let's talk inside."

I followed him down the white hallway toward the dining room, passing his wife Tilda, who sat at a computer in the shadowy office, planning a South African Evangelical Mission. Tilda ignored my hello.

Bard and I sat at his dining room table, on heavy chairs with clawed feet and cream-coloured seats. He ran his big paw across the table's finish. "Burr walnut. Queen Anne." I didn't know what that meant—but someone had polished the table and chairs to gleam like trophies, and I knew the set was worth more than everything I'd ever owned.

But in a room of antiques, vases, and porcelain figurines, what really interested me was a pink, half-baked clay bust staring at me from the fireplace mantel. Bard caught me looking at the strange sculpture.

"Miriam made it in school," he said. "It's Mordecai Richler."

Miriam was the youngest daughter—a fifteen-year-old bookworm who sometimes followed me around the farm the way my little sister used to when we were kids. Miriam wanted to talk books with me ever since I'd told her I had dropped out of university to become a writer. Her bust looked nothing like Mordecai Richler.

"David, our little Miriam has a—sometimes inappropriate—imagination." His grin was gone. "While you're working here, we'd appreciate it if you only interacted with your coworkers."

There was kindness in Bard's eyes, something that made me believe it was Tilda who had put him up to this. Miriam had told me that her mother always worried about what the migrant workers and I were up to—said it kept her up at night, and that the doctor had given her pills for that.

"Bard, Miriam and I only talk about books. She's been telling me about *Franny and Zooey*."

From the office, Tilda snapped, "That's not *all* they talk about!"

Bard sighed. "You've had unsuitable conversations with Miriam."

"Huh? I'm not sure—"

"Suicide?"

The room descended into silence, the silence of apprehension—the silence before people are fired.

I tried to squirm out of it with a chuckle, hoping to lighten up the room. "We discussed *hypotheticals*... if we *had* to... All the guys answered."

"Did you tell her how you would do it?"

I couldn't lie. "Yeah. I said I'd lay in the forest, some Tool blasting through headphones, and rest my head on a stick of dynamite. Or I'd sit on the edge of a skyscraper..." I held a finger-gun to my temple. "And I'd pull the trigger, toward the street."

Bard shook his head. "I don't understand."

"If I survived the gunshot, I'd at least be unconscious for—"

He held his hand up. A stop signal. "That conversation does not reflect well on you. Please limit your interactions while you work here."

That was it.

I wasn't fired.

I followed Bard back down the creaking hallway and didn't bother saying goodbye to Tilda. I guess we weren't speaking anymore. I'd never seen Tilda talk to the Mexican workers, either. I assumed she was the reason Oscar, their eighty-pound German Shepherd, always growled at them.

As I walked out into the yard, I thought of our truck driver, Mark, a potbellied creep from their church. He'd gone to jail for molesting his cousins—seven- and nine-year-old girls—and everyone on the farm knew about it. With a guy like him around, I wondered how they got so paranoid about Miriam's harmless crush on me.

"Mark's the guy you need to keep an eye on," I said.

Bard stayed behind his screen door. "This isn't about Mark. He repented. God pardoned him."

I didn't argue.

•

In the dewy, green rows, the guys and I chased the tractor as it rumbled, hauling its squeaky, fifty-year-old wagon. We wielded bolo machetes and harvested two broccoli rows each—a dozen Mexicans and me, the *güero*.

The fastest cutters occupied two stations in an eight-foot gap between the tractor and trailer because if you fell behind there, you'd end up under the trailer. When we'd first started harvesting, I'd struggled to keep up anywhere, but I'd worked my way to the front rows with Ignacio weeks ago.

Ignacio Hernandez-Hernandez. That was his name because both his parents' surnames were Hernandez. He swore they were unrelated. Ignacio was forty-five, slim and muscular with blue eyes, pale skin, and a thick black moustache. He looked nothing like the rest of the Mexican workers, but he was a real *ranchero* who owned a farm back home, somewhere outside Mazatlán. Three cows, two horses, eight hens, and two roosters, all running around on twenty acres he left in his wife's hands when he came to work on Bard's farm for minimum wage.

We chatted every day, through the verdant fields, in the sun and rain, or over chess games after dinner. Ignacio got a kick out of my Spanish—said I sounded Mexican. I'm French-Canadian, so the languages are similar to me, and rather than studying Spanish, I acquired it just by travelling and listening. So, I listened to Ignacio a lot, and after a while, started to wonder what my life would have been like if he were my father.

"Bard and Tilda think I'm a pedophile," I said.

Ignacio cracked up.

"Don't laugh. This job's degrading. I should be writing more, anyway." I spotted a ripe broccoli, and in one motion, decapitated the plant, tore off its leaves, and flung the head through the air in a satisfying arc into the moving trailer—then on to the next plant.

Ignacio kept his head down as he hunted ripe broccoli. "If you want to travel and write all winter, you have to slave now."

Ignacio knew that while working on the farm, I had been writing a novella called *Curriculum Vitae*—an account of every dead-end job I'd endured. Chapter One delved into my career delivering flyers as a ten-year-old, an occupation I entertained for two hours, hauling a giant sack of advertisements from door to door, until I realized I could dump handfuls into each garbage can I came across, and eventually half the bag into a construction dumpster. Chapter Two: Sixteen hours as an office custodian. Chapter Three: Shopping-cart collector in an Australian shopping-mall parking lot ridden with huge spiders. The final chapter, Seventeen, would recount my time on the farm.

The little manuscript had generated so much self-confidence that I'd hired Bella Chevalier, editor-in-chief of Edifice Books in Toronto. She wasn't a complete stranger; I had held a door open for her the previous winter when I worked at an auction house in Toronto (Chapter Fifteen). She was a tall, graceful woman with long, black hair. She wore a full-length wool coat, black and double-breasted with a tightly cinched waist. She'd arrived with her hands in her flap pockets, so I'd held the door for her. After the fine arts auctioneer, Paul Orr, told me who she was, I kept my gaze on her all night and thought: one day, she'll open the door for me. Now, in an effort to create a deadline that would obligate me to write, I had wired Bella Chevalier five hundred dollars in advance, and we'd agreed I would send my completed manuscript to her in March.

"We all have to slave, so we may as well slave over what we love," Ignacio said. "To write, you'll have to slave over books, dictionaries, keyboards… You'll screw your eyes up and lose all your friends. But it'll be worth it, 'cause even if you wanted to do nothing with your life, you'd have to be a slave to laziness."

"What does that mean?"

"It means next to success, the best thing in life is to be a total failure."

I didn't agree with him about all of us having to slave, but he got me thinking of hanging on to my job a little longer, since I had only saved two thousand dollars.

"Why don't you come work part-time on my farm this winter?" Ignacio asked. "We can only pay you room and board, but we have a cabin you can sleep in. I even have an old typewriter you can use."

"That's a nice offer, but I think I'd rather be in Costa Rica."

While I was working on the farm, my old friend Mac's mother had died of bone cancer. After her funeral, he had flown to Costa Rica and rented a house on the beach. It seemed important for me to spend the winter down there. Mac said he had an extra room to rent.

"Won't going there be too expensive?"

"You're just trying to get me to work on your farm."

He laughed. "Yes, but not for my benefit."

"Thanks, but I'll be alright."

•

I was driving the tractor through the field one morning, with the back window open so I could hear the guys following all around the trailer, when news came over the radio that two airplanes had flown into the World Trade Center. I stopped the tractor, turned the radio up, and leaned over my seat to tell the guys what I was hearing. You never forget the way fifteen men look up at you when you tell them the South Tower has collapsed, then the North Tower. We were an eight-hour drive from New York, and yet they looked scared.

At night, alone in the small office behind the greenhouses, I watched the footage. I heard the witnesses talk about the people they saw jumping out of the burning buildings after waving their white shirts. They'd known their fate and surrendered. It made me think of my father, declining the cancer treatment that would have only postponed his death. Then I thought, I'd better not talk about any of this with Miriam.

•

In October, the overnight frost crept into cold mornings, and there was hardly anything left to harvest in the fields. One night, I drove the guys into the city in our fifteen-passenger van. While the rest of us went shopping, Ignacio went for a beer at the Chinese restaurant with Juan-Carlos, the youngest of the migrant workers—a quiet guy who never said much except to make perverted jokes.

I spotted them eating chicken wings with Rita. She was a stocky, older woman with curly, grey hair and thick glasses. She worked on the farm part time packing broccoli. They were all red-eyed, and Rita seemed to like Juan-Carlos sitting with his arm around her.

"Dave," she said. "Are you avoiding Miriam?"

"It's David," I said.

She didn't hear me. I had a way of speaking too quietly whenever I got nervous, like I didn't want people to hear what I had to say.

Rita grinned like a child with a secret. "Miriam wants to know if you're interested. She thinks you've been avoiding her."

"What do you mean, *interested*? She's fifteen. I'm twenty-four." I looked to Ignacio and Juan-Carlos for support, but they only understood Spanish.

Rita held her hand to her chest. "Oh, it's just puppy love... So, you're not interested?"

"No! She's a *child*! Why would you ask me that?" I turned to the guys and rattled my keys. "*¿Están listos?*"

"*Me cortas los vuelos,*" Juan-Carlos said. "She's getting me drunk. She might take me home."

I looked into Rita's drooping eyes, knowing she couldn't understand what Juan-Carlos had said. "You know, she's got grandchildren," I said, in Spanish.

"*Siéntate,*" Ignacio said. He grabbed my wrist a little too hard.

I pulled my hand away. "You guys can walk back; it'll sober you up."

•

In the morning, Juan-Carlos wasn't there. Ignacio said he'd left him at the restaurant and walked home alone.

Bard entered the shop and said, "I got a call from the police. They arrested Juan-Carlos at a gas station last night. He groped the young lady working there—kissed her and tried to shove his hand down her pants."

I translated for Ignacio, then we stood there, not knowing what to say. It was awkward the way I'd left him at the bar, but I guess neither of us wanted to talk about it, so we never did.

And we never saw Juan-Carlos again.

•

I was writing in the greenhouse office one evening when Miriam slipped in and hopped onto the deep freezer in her cut-at-the-knee jean shorts.

"I sculpted your head in art class," she said. Her innocent smile revealed the gaps between her buck teeth. "Don't worry. I told my parents it was Mordecai Richler so they wouldn't get all weird about it."

In the monitor glow reflected off Miriam's thick glasses, I could see myself trapped and terrified of her parents finding us alone. "I've never read Mordecai Richler." I stood to flip the light switch, just as the door opened.

It was Bard.

His voice fired like a machine gun. "Miriam, this is a workspace!"

Miriam slid off the freezer and scurried out of the office.

My voice squeaked. "I was trying to write."

Bard shook his head. "This office is off-limits after work hours." He slammed the door shut.

The next morning, I heard the guys climb out of their bunk beds. Looking out the frosty window, at the stars hung in astronomical twilight, I knew it would be another wet day in the mud. I thought of seeing Bard again, then hid my head under the pillow and asked one of the guys to turn off the light when they left the room. I fell asleep, but woke again when Ignacio came in.

"¿*Que haces*?"

"I'm sick," I said. "I ate some bad broccoli."

"You're not sick."

"Can you tell Bard I can't work today?"

"What about the money?"

"I can't work for someone who thinks I'm a pedophile. He won't even let me write in the office anymore."

"Talk to him."

"I'm quitting."

"At least tell him why you're leaving. Say goodbye."

"Goodbyes are overrated."

"Don't burn your bridges."

That was the last thing Ignacio said. If he had pushed a little harder, maybe I would have gone to work—because I would have eventually listened to him. But he didn't, because he wasn't my father.

So, when the van and the tractor drove off, it was time. I smoked a bowl in the washroom, then snuck into the greenhouse office to call a cab to take me to the bus station, and while I waited, I printed the first sixteen chapters of *Curriculum Vitae*, single-spaced, cramming it all onto fifty pages.

CHAPTER TWO

I left Canada on my twenty-fifth birthday. A driveaway service in Toronto hired me to deliver a car to a couple of snowbirds in Sarasota, Florida. The car service covered gas and paid three hundred dollars. If I slept in the car, I could use the three hundred dollars to make my way down to Central America.

Seeing nothing to write about along the interstates, I just kept driving. For three days, I ate drive-thru burgers, drank coffee, and parked at rest stops where I slept very little, determined to reach warm weather and Mac.

We'd gone to the same junior high-school, but he'd probably never noticed me then. At thirteen, he was the only kid in our schoolyard who wore a leather jacket. He had long, blond hair in a ponytail, and he smoked and drank. I remember some girls on the bus talking about how hot he was, which I didn't understand because Mac was skinny with a big nose. But he grew up with two older brothers, and I think that's what made him act older and self-assured, and that's what people liked about him.

When I was seventeen, weeks after my father had died of pancreatic cancer, I'd run into Mac at a house party. I hadn't seen him in four years, but he still had his blonde ponytail. He sat on the floor with a bottle of beer and someone's acoustic guitar. He talked to me about

Nietzsche's *Übermensch*, began calling me *Slim*, then played and sang a slowed-down cover of Nine Inch Nails' *Down in It*. Afterwards, Mac said he'd heard about my father. We got drunk together and talked about how futile it had been for my father to have slaved for a mining company for twenty years, only to die at forty. We talked of leaving our hometown—fearing the predictability of our lives if we stayed.

Even though Mac was only ten months older than me, I started to follow him around like a little brother. All my life, I'd wanted an older brother. Before I was born, my mother had had a miscarriage, so I had to be the bigger brother to my sister—a role for which I'd always felt unqualified.

I'd followed Mac to Ottawa for college, but we drank too much to make our classes. By then, he already had a stomach ulcer from too much hard liquor, but that didn't stop him. I later followed him to Australia for a winter and then we'd moved to Toronto, and somewhere in there I started writing and thinking of Mac as some larger-than-life character for my stories—someone whose rebellious convictions inspired me to live a life worth writing about.

So, on the way to Costa Rica, I thought about Mac and what awaited us. I also thought about his poor mother—remembering the scars on her sternum from her first cancer. Mostly, I thought about how Mac and I could get drunk and talk about our dead parents.

•

I arrived at a gated community in Florida. The guard, perched in his gatehouse, eyeballed me like I planned to rob the place.

I parked at the unit, lugged my backpack to the door, and rang the bell. I waited a while, sweat dripping down my back, until I walked around the house and found the old couple slouched in lawn chairs, drinking iced tea, glistening like glazed hams.

"The car service told me you're going down to Costa Rica," the wife said, taking the car keys from me. "If you go by Cancun, I highly recommend you catch the Captain Hook dinner show."

"Captain Hook?" I asked. "Like the Robin Hood character?"

"Peter Pan, silly." She walked off. "I have to run to the bank to pay you. Have some carrots."

I dropped my backpack and sat in the lawn chair next to her husband. He had thin, grey hair parted to the side and wet with sweat, and he wore sunglasses with mirrored lenses.

He pointed at my backpack, bloated with my sleeping bag, tent, camp stove, clothes, hiking boots, books, pens, notepads, mini tape recorder, and my fifty pages. "Where'd you say you're off to, son?"

"Malpaís, Costa Rica."

"Oh? Fantastic birdwatching that way." The old guy slurped his drink, then rambled about tanagers and motmots, and other birds nobody's heard about. "How long you there for?"

"For the winter."

"You got a job down there?"

"No. I'm meeting my buddy, Mac. And I'm writing a book."

His lips twitched, as if the words were ready to come out before his brain had decided what those words would be. "I could write a book. I have a way with words.

You give me a crossword and I'll knock it off in half an hour. Ask the wife."

"Will she be gone much longer? I need a lift to the bus station."

"What are you gonna write about?"

I grabbed a warm carrot and watched the sweat roll down the bridge of his nose and drip onto his shorts. "Oh, about a farm where I worked. I lived there with sixteen Mexicans—well, one of them went to jail."

"What for?"

"He assaulted a woman at a gas station."

"Why would you want to write about dirt like that? I hope you have a job waiting for you back home." The way he said "job" reminded me of my father.

Now he straightened himself on his lawn chair and peered over his sunglasses at me with eyes like dull, grey pebbles. "Son, it's good you want to write, but when the little Chinese come over, one of them'll take your job."

"They can have my job."

I didn't even get a laugh out of him. He shook his head. "Gotta work hard while you can, son."

I looked at the guy, and thought, he'll never write a book, but if he did, I wouldn't want to read it and someone like Bella Chevalier wouldn't either. I mean, what's so hard about holding on to a job? Try holding on to a dream.

CHAPTER THREE

I would have saved a lot of time and money if the driveaway service had set me up with a car destined for Texas or New Mexico. Instead, for three days I rode buses around the Gulf Coast—north to Tallahassee, then west and back down toward Brownsville. TVs inundated the bus stations with news that American soldiers were in Afghanistan. The passengers seemed to look to the televisions for assurance they could soon go back to their game shows, sports, and sitcoms—to regularly scheduled programming—and stop considering anything outside personal limitations.

For me, the news had hardly any effect. I'd spent so much of my time pulling my feet out from the quicksand of our culture that I thought if the whole structure crumpled, I might even be better off. I might thrive. So, while a K-9 unit slobbered over my bags, I just studied a framed interstate map on the wall, running my finger across the I-10 to Brownsville and imagining starting over—all variations of my life—all the potential characters waiting to be written about, in mysterious places like Spanish Fort, Moss Point, De Lisle, Rose City, or Riviera.

On the bus, I tried to read and tried to sleep, balling up my sweater for a pillow, but mostly, I scribbled notes about the people around me, like the pretty blonde with ruffled pixie hair and a Southern accent who got on in Pensacola and sat across the aisle. Her sweet voice trembled as she explained to the old woman between us that a new makeup magazine sales job awaited her in Biloxi, Mississippi. I imagined sitting beside her and convincing her to forget about her job and come along to Costa Rica. But when the old woman left, the empty seat seemed to ridicule me, and my courage seeped away.

I fell asleep, and when I woke, she was gone. In her seat was an elderly woman with her face hidden under a dark shawl. She held a rosary and recited prayers over and over. I imagined her shadowy mumbles begging her God to watch over us all.

Outside Tallahassee one night, I woke when someone shouted, "I'll shoot you in yer goddamned mouth!"

No one on the bus made much of a fuss about this outburst, but I pulled my hood over my head as if it might shield me from a bullet.

In Baton Rouge, a man argued with police outside the bus. I turned on my recorder.

"But it ain't yours! I don't care. It ain't yours! I want my fucking knife!" The man stormed onto the bus and up the aisle. He wore a black mesh tank-top and had a thin, black moustache; he looked like he was on his way to a costume party, dressed like Freddy Mercury. He shouted toward the door, "I ain't no bin Laden! What would I want to kill my own people for? It's a double-serrated knife, for God's sake!" He dropped in the seat next to me and muttered, "I live in Tucson, Arizona, goddamnit. I *need* a knife!" He tapped my shoulder. "Am I right?"

I nodded, comforted he no longer had a knife. All I had was a cheap steak knife I'd stolen from the farm because I'd lost my camping utensils somewhere. "Did you say double-serrated?" I don't know why I asked him that.

He tilted his head to me because he couldn't hear me. "What'd you say?"

"Your knife. You said it was double-serrated?"

"Damn right."

"That's cool, man."

CHAPTER FOUR

In Brownsville, Texas, I stepped off the bus and hurried through the rain without a map. I got lost searching for the border crossing to Matamoros. By the time I found it, off East University Boulevard, it was closed, and my socks and backpack were soaked.

I checked into a cheap hotel by the border. Twenty bucks for a room that smelled like a wet dog, with a purple bed and pink wallpaper—torn and scrawled upon with markers and pens. The shower stall was half-pulled off the wall, and when I pried it open, I could peer into the empty room next door.

I slept on the sunken, springy mattress, which felt like something salvaged from a scrapyard. I dreamed I stood in line at a bookstore. Voices behind me called my name. A horde of pale, sickly individuals approached and grasped at me. "Touch me! Hold me. Hold my hand." I spread my arms wide for them, because I understood: I was a healer.

Something woke me.

I lay on my back, my feet crossed and my arms outstretched like Jesus on his cross. A light poured onto me like a holy spotlight. It was the hallway light, shining through the transom window.

A man shouted from the hallway, "Let me go! No. No!"

I grabbed my recorder, moved the desk chair to the door, and stood on it on the tips of my toes. The window was still too high up for me to see directly outside my door, so I held up the recorder instead and recorded audio of two policemen arresting a Mexican man. One cop kept saying, "Back to Mexico. Bye-bye, *gabacho*."

"Please! I did *no* do *anyting*! Sir!"

A struggle. Something slammed against my door. When they moved farther down the hallway, I saw the two policemen dragging the man down the stairs. He sobbed and kicked the walls, and his blue boxer shorts fell halfway off his ass. I wanted something to stop them. I wanted the lights to go out, an earthquake—anything—to let the man run free. Instead, he vanished. Back in bed, I wondered if the man had spent his life savings to pay a *coyote* to squeeze him through a hole in the fence—to drag himself across the desert and claw his way into the very life I would have happily given him.

CHAPTER FIVE

In the morning, I crossed the bridge over the Rio Grande. The Mexican colours unfolded like spring. There was Norteña music, car horns, locals shouting, and megaphones strapped to cars that senselessly blared, *"¡Helotés! ¡Gas! ¡Camaroneeeees!"*

For five pesos, a street vendor sold me fresh-squeezed orange juice in a bag with a straw. An old man sold juicy tacos *a la barbacoa* off his tailgate for six pesos. Leaning against his white pickup, he swung a plastic bag around in the shade. I ordered two, and sat on his tailgate. For some reason, I remembered a dream I'd had the night before—my father seated on our sofa, hunched over and frail—the sunken cheeks of his dying body. I'd sat beside him. "Dad, you're dying. You have to talk to us." But he looked ahead, lost, vacant, already someplace else. I sobbed and shouted, over and over: "Dad!" But he wouldn't answer, and I woke in tears as I often had.

I snapped out of it when the old man shouted to the gas station attendant across the street, *"¡Ànimo, huevón...apurate!"*

The attendant, busy cleaning a car windshield, looked back and shouted some Spanish jargon unknown to me. The old man cracked up and shouted, *"¡Señor, le dijieron que se baña, pero no lo hizo!"* The attendant looked around, then grabbed his balls. The old man laughed again and gave him the finger.

"You know him?" I asked.

"No, but I see him every day. We tease each other just to pass the time."

"There's always time in Mexico," I said.

The old man nodded, but I don't think he really knew what I was talking about.

•

I splurged a hundred and fifty dollars on first-class bus tickets all the way to San José, Costa Rica. Over three or four days, we rode down the Gulf Coast Plains, across the Sierra Madre de Chiapas, and into Central America. In the comforts of air conditioning, snacks, tinted windows, and reclining seats with a leg rest, I read and made notes on my manuscript.

Chapter Ten was a favourite. The Button Factory:

> *With resume in hand, I entered the quiet warehouse around 9 AM. A white-haired man with skinny legs and a fat belly read my resume and said, "You sound like a smart guy. How about we start you today?" Minutes later, I was up a ladder in a dark, narrow aisle of dusty pallet racking.*
>
> *The entire warehouse was rows and rows of boxes—large boxes, small boxes, shoe boxes—everything filled with buttons. I'd been handed an order sheet, and had to find the various button numbers and meet the required*

quantities of buttons: 200 x #3123, 100 x #1211, 400 x #5333.

An hour in, an argument erupted. The boss shouted, "Why would you do it like that?"

"That's how Petersen does it," someone said.

"Petersen? He's just a stupid as you are! Goddamnit! There's a cancer in this place, and I'm gonna cure it!"

Finally, it was break time. Everyone disappeared. I wandered toward the break room, hoping the change in my pocket was enough to buy a drink and a snack from the vending machine. But a delivery truck driver stopped me. He stood beside a couple of loaded pallets.

"Can you sign for this?"

"Hang on," I said. "I just started. Let me check with the boss."

I approached the boss in the hallway. When I asked if I should sign for the delivery, or if he wanted to look it over, he said, "What do you think, smart guy? Of course you sign it! After break, you're going to do inventory."

I followed him to a board on the wall, where keys hung. He gave me a key. "You'll go into that warehouse out back, find the inventory binder—see if you can figure it out and pick up where they left off, smart guy."

I skipped break, thinking, I'll show him, and walked outside to the smaller cinder block warehouse. But when I stuck the key in the doorknob and turned, the key broke in half. After failing to pry it out, I thought, there's no way I can go back inside to tell the boss the key broke. So, I dropped the other half to the ground and climbed over the fence that led to the Dufferin Street sidewalk.

I walked home with a smile, imagining that cranky boss finding the broken key in the knob and thinking I'd done it on purpose.

•

I arrived in San José, Costa Rica at 6 a.m. It wasn't the Central America I'd come to expect—too many American fast-food chains, clothing stores, modern buildings, and clean-shaven parks. Plastered everywhere were the words, *¡Pura Vida!* And when I came across a poster for a birdwatching tour in San Gerardo de Dota, I'd seen enough, so I rode a taxi to Puntarenas, planning to take a ferry to the Nicoya Peninsula the next day.

In Puntarenas, I checked into a quiet hostel, where a young Israeli checking out sold me a gram of weed for about ten bucks. Later, I held the door open for a long-haired brunette who carried a small, green backpack with a Canadian flag patch. I offered a shy smile and said hello, but she didn't hear me. She had that tense look on her face that said she was lost.

Inside, she waited at the front desk. I kept an eye on her while pretending to read brochures on a cork board. Monkey Park. Kayaking tours. She stammered through her broken Spanish, assembling a sentence for the security guy covering for the front desk clerk. Neither of us understood her.

"I speak Spanish," I said.

A sigh of relief from the woman. "Thanks."

"*Esta buscando un cuarto*," I said.

The man fetched a ledger. "Ahh, *pues sí hay, sí hay*."

"There's room," I said.

She wrenched off her backpack, and it hit the floor with a weary thud. "Oh gosh, that's great. I thought I'd be out there in the dark."

"*¿Cuantas noches?*" the man asked.

"*Una.*" She winked at me. "I got that one." She lay her passport on the counter. Violet Gladstone. 5'11". She had an inch on me, with perfect posture—looked like a teacher, someone with a pension.

I stood up tall. "I'm David."

No response. But why? Had I not broken the ice? Perhaps she'd been too absorbed in counting her money to hear me, or so used to men swarming her that she could ignore me the way a monk can ignore a fly. Either way, I refused to stand there and make a fool of myself waiting for her attention, so I blurted, *"Buenas noches,"* and hurried upstairs to my room, but left the door half-open.

When I heard Violet creak up the stairs, I tried to tame my hair, plucked my dirty socks off the bed, flung them across the room, and sat up straight on the bed, holding a copy of the *Tico Times*.

A gentle knock at my door.

I laid down the paper as Violet nudged the door open. "Thanks again for helping."

"No problem."

Silence.

Say something to her, you jerk, I thought. Something clever, something affable.

"I saw the flag on your bag," I said. "I'm from Canada, too."

She smiled—a real smile—like she recognized me.

We went out to a local restaurant with a blue taxidermy fish hung on a neon-green wall. Three German men drank at the bar, laughing and talking too loud under the palapa roof. Violet and I sat at a tall table in the middle of the room and ordered *Gallo Pinto* and Imperial beer.

Sitting across from me, she fanned herself with the paper menu. "Shoot, it's so hot here."

The way she never swore, but said, "shoot," "darn it," and "gosh," Violet reminded me of Chantal Lacroix, a girlfriend I'd had in junior high. The year before, I'd been back in my hometown, stoned out of my head while seated in my dentist's waiting room, when in walked Chantal Lacroix. I hadn't seen her in eleven years. She carried a baby, and probably didn't recognize me with my long hair, because she sat right beside me and didn't say anything. I was too high to speak or even look at her. Anyway, she was raising a child. What could we have possibly talked about?

"You don't say much, do you?" Violet asked.

I shook my head, and she laughed. I ordered another beer to get a buzz on and find the courage to talk.

"What do you do in Canada?" she asked.

"I worked on a farm this summer."

"That's cool."

"Not really. What do you do?"

"Guess," she said.

"Substitute teacher?"

"Nope."

"Nurse?"

"No. I'm a flight attendant."

I could see Violet in her uniform—the flight attendant who leans over your armrest to force the overhead compartments closed, and brushes your arm with her hip. Yes, that one. The flight attendant you'd run to if the plane went down, the one you'd squeeze as you plummeted to the sea.

"Is that why you're here?" I asked, thinking I could hang around with her for another day or two—maybe take her to see the monkeys I'd read about in the brochures. "You fly into San José for work?"

She looked outside, as if the answer were out there watching her. The sun had set, and she had taken her sunglasses off, but she put them on again. Her cheeks were red, and I could tell she was crying under there.

She sniffled. Then she laughed.

"What's wrong?" I asked.

"I flew into San José with my boyfriend. But we split up."

Split up, as in break up? "What's he like?" Probably an accountant—someone who doesn't read Henry Miller or cut his own hair.

"Tom? He's forty. Anyway, we had a fight and...before I took a bus here, I spent two nights alone in a hotel watching *The Bachelor,* wondering how I got mixed up with a guy fifteen years older than me. I don't know. I still want to go to the peninsula. It was my idea. Can I come to the peninsula with you? Your Spanish is kinda useful."

As casually as I could muster, I said, "By all means."

•

We picked up four cans of beer from the corner store beside our hostel, then we sat alone on the hostel's communal balcony overlooking the woeful street.

I finished my second beer and lobbed the empty can into the garbage.

"You want the last one?" she asked.

"Thanks," I said. "I have a bit of weed. You want to smoke?"

"No thanks," she said. "But knock yourself out."

"Shit. You wouldn't happen to have rolling papers?"

She shook her head.

I pulled a beer can out of the garbage, then folded a dent in the can and poked holes through it with the tip of my pen.

"What are you doing?"

"Making a pipe." I looked up at her, expecting applause for my ingenuity.

"You're gonna burn aluminum in your lungs?"

The flame lit the balcony with a red glow. The can burned hot. The dry weed cooked my throat. I coughed so much I drooled on myself, but thankfully, it was too dark for Violet to notice. I tried to remember a joke to tell her. But I only knew crude jokes with punchlines like, "You think I wished for a twelve-inch pianist?" And then I was stoned, swallowed into a shell that sank to the warm bottom of my mind, where I needed nobody.

I saw a slow shooting star burn directly in front of us. "Did you see that?"

She sat with her feet up on her chair, her arms wrapped around her legs and her head on her knees. "What?"

"Nothing..."

She stood from her chair and yawned. "I'm going to bed."

"Goodnight," I said, thinking I would never see her again.

"See you tomorrow," she said.

•

In the dewy morning air, we waited on the dock for the ferry. Small waves sputtered toward us, carrying foam and tangled seaweed and the raw ocean smell. Violet followed when I climbed over the handrails and walked onto the rocks. A hermit crab hid in a crevasse, and I lured it out with a stick, which it pinched at with its tiny claws.

Violet crouched beside me. "What is it?"

"Breakfast."

When she saw the crab, she rested her head on my shoulder. "Aw, don't hurt it."

"I won't hurt it. I just want to see it."

Her hair smelled like the hostel shampoo—a kids' shampoo bottle someone had left behind—*champú de durazno*. It smelled exactly like peaches, and had me craving peach juice. I felt the silent weight of Violet's head and wondered how much of that weight was made up of her ex, Tom.

•

From the ferry, we rode an old school bus to Malpaís. When the bus drove off, we could hear the crash of the ocean through the jungle—trees with giant, green teardrop leaves and eerie fig trees with exposed roots that dug into the ground like tangled needles.

We walked up the dirt road and arrived at a property with a hand-painted sign that read: *SE RENTA CABINAS*. An older woman swept the stone path. She led us to three rustic cabins behind her house, then unlocked the padlock on one and flipped the switch to turn on a bulb hung from the ceiling. The musty cabin had a table and chair, a gas burner, a sink and counter, a bar fridge, and two double beds.

"*Diez mil colones,*" she said. "*O, quieren sus proprias cabinas?*"

"What did she say?" Violet asked.

The woman had said the cabins cost ten thousand *colones* a night, and asked if we wanted our own cabins. Thirty dollars was ridiculous, and there were two beds, so I said, "She said it's the last cabin available."

Violet shrugged. "Okay."

•

I worried about running into Mac. Violet was too well-mannered to bring around someone like him. So I kept my head down when we walked to the general store in our flip-flops and pasty white feet. We bought bananas, eggs, pasta, sauce, bread, butter, and a bottle of red wine, and I bought a can of peach nectar and rolling papers.

After dinner, Violet and I walked to the beach. We smoked a joint while we drank from the wine bottle and watched the sun set over the ocean. Eight-foot waves thundered in the dark, and the breeze wafted salty vapor at us. Violet wrapped her hands around my arm and put her head on my shoulder again. Was I the only one concerned about her boyfriend? Was she too stoned, or drunk on half a bottle of wine? I'll pull away, I thought. That would be the right thing to do.

But she pulled her head away first. "I like cozy shoulders." She stood and peeled her clothes off and ran to the water. "You comin'?"

Glowing in the moonlight, her beautiful white ass beckoned me.

I tore off my clothes and ran with my hard-on stabbing the air.

We hurled ourselves into the whitewash.

"What did the beach say to the ocean?" she asked.

"What?"

"Long tide no *sea*!"

I laughed. "That's not funny."

When the wave rolled back, we stood naked and faced each other. Her hair dripped over her wet, slender body sparkling like the stars. I stood there with my stubborn boner.

"Um, so I still have a boyfriend."

"I know." I dove into a wave. When I finally came up, I dragged myself out of the water and walked to my clothes. I wanted to forget about Violet. I wanted to find Mac at a bar, where he would certainly be.

Violet came close and pressed her body to mine.

I held her tight.

"I bet you're a good kisser," she said.

•

At the cabin, Violet had it her way—shoving me onto the bed and tearing off my shorts. She jumped onto me and screamed so loud I had to smother her mouth with my hand and say, "Shhh! They'll call the police."

She bit my finger and shrieked in laughter as the sweat and seawater coursed down her body and dripped all over me. Thoughts of her boyfriend and the landlady disappeared. Our plane was on fire.

"Oh my God!" she shouted. Her body quivered. "I can't feel my hands!" She dropped her head on my chest, and we laughed as though we knew each other—old friends, old lovers, ex-lovers, whatever. She rolled off me, pulled the wet sheet over her shoulder, and turned away.

I slid my hand over her hip, and she flinched like it burned.

"Please don't," she said.

Her hair on the pillow had become a dark, impenetrable veil.

•

In the morning, I woke to the sound of Violet slipping on her shoes. Her backpack leaned against the door. Even with a guilty, panicked look on her face, she'd never looked prettier.

"I'm heading up to Manzanillo," she said.

I didn't have to ask. I knew her boyfriend was in Manzanillo. I sat up and fumbled around the bed and found my wet shorts twisted up in the sheets. The sand on the bed scratched like shattered glass. I got up and hugged her. She felt soft and empty, like a stranger.

She opened the door and stepped outside.

"You sure you don't want breakfast?" I asked. "I'll make eggs."

"No, that's okay. I have a banana." It sounded so sad, the way she said it. Afterwards, she just walked away without a goodbye.

Later, traipsing through ferns and mud in my swim shorts, I walked down a trail that led to the white-sand beach. The sun pelted my pale skin as I crossed the hot sand. I played in the waves and made crazy plans to follow Violet to Manzanillo, but when I sat in the sand, squinting at the ocean, her presence—along with any romantic urge I had—evaporated from me like a droplet of sea in the sun.

CHAPTER SIX

Malpaís and Santa Teresa shared one dirt road. I found the green-looking house with mossy wood siding that Mac had described in an email. A 'room for rent' sign hung on the rusty gate, and a tattered hammock sagged over the porch like a giant cobweb.

I walked up the front stairs, which were covered in chicken shit. An old dining table was scattered with beer cans and ashes. A chicken ran across the porch and leaped off.

The front door was open, and from inside played Junior Brown's "Highway Patrol." I poked my head in. "*¿Hola?*" Faded sheets draped the windows of a front room furnished with a chair, two milk crates, and various motorcycle parts. A beaten-down acoustic guitar stood in the corner, with half its strings popped and drooping onto the floor. The place smelled like a hamster coop.

I walked deeper. The music was coming from the back room. The kitchen sink was loaded with dirty dishes and scraps of food. The counter spilled over with more beer cans, more ashes, and several empty dime bags. The tiny washroom looked abandoned—a filthy floor, moldy shower curtain, and a shower encrusted with grime. I became certain I had the wrong house—because Mac wouldn't live this way—and that if I ventured to the open door at the end of the hallway, I'd find an angry local in bed with his crack pipe. I turned to leave, and caught my terrified expression in the mirror. But tucked in the corner of the frame, covered in toothpaste splatter, was a black-and-white photo of Mac's mother, her timid smile captured forever.

I tiptoed down the hallway toward the open door.

And in the bedroom, tangled in the bedsheet with a blue-haired woman, was Mac in his worn-out boxers.

I cracked up laughing. "Shit. Sorry."

He spun off the bed violently and landed on his feet with the sheet wrapped around him.

Then he recognized me. "Oh, it's you, Slim! Thank God."

"Hi, I'm Milla," the woman said in a Scandinavian accent. "I'm naked."

I didn't even realize Mac had torn the sheet off her body. I backed into the hallway until she fell out of sight.

"I was only letting you know," she called out. "I don't mind."

Mac didn't seem to mind either. His skinny frame staggered past me, and I followed him to the fridge. He snatched two beer cans and handed me one. He looked at me through pupils so big and black, they looked like stickers.

•

After Milla dressed and left, Mac and I sat on his porch, drinking our beers.

"What's her story?" I asked.

"She's from Finland. I met her last week in the cereal aisle at the grocery store. I saw her pink boots and said, 'Nice boots.' An hour later, we banged in her boyfriend's bed."

"Her *boyfriend's* bed?"

"Yeah, some surfer dude... I scored a bunch of pills from her, too. Some Percocet, Vicodin, and a bunch of blow, too."

"I don't want to get into that stuff."

"Shit's pure down here, Slim. They ship it in cans from Colombia."

I felt uneasy about Mac getting into the stuff again because I'd been to enough parties where the conversations had been drained of imagination, intellect, and laughter because we'd done lines, and they'd all started talking big while I sat quietly with my thoughts screaming in my head.

"Where's your room for rent?" I asked.

Mac pointed to a small, empty storage room on the porch. There was nothing in there but a cot. "No door on it, so security's not a feature."

We agreed if I took care of cleaning, I could rent the room for a hundred bucks a month. Then Mac pinched two pills off the table—one dark blue, one light blue—and swallowed them with beer.

"Should you mix those with beer?"

He eyed me sideways and walked back to the fridge, letting out a strange cackle I'd never heard.

•

Mac worked part time at Las Olas, a small bar on the beach—a concrete pad resting among the palm and coconut trees. It looked like a film set with its Tiki decor, bamboo furniture, and thatched roof. Behind the bar, there were spotlights that, in the evening, would illuminate the Jurassic-sized tropical plant leaves.

Mac's job was to sleep in a hammock slung across the dance floor and guard the bar overnight. They'd given him a rusty machete for protection. He said the job paid him enough to cover his expenses. In the seven years I'd known him, Mac had always gone hard while still keeping his shit together. He'd been making a thousand dollars a week as a TV production manager for the last two years. So I didn't understand why he wanted or needed a job that required him to sleep in a hammock with a machete.

The bar owner was Allen, a half-American, half-Mexican man who Mac knew from Toronto. With his slicked-back hair and long, dark face, Allen resembled Humphrey Bogart. He smoked cigarettes, but never blew the smoke out; instead, he let it seep out of his mouth as he spoke. When I told Allen I'd come here with a girl I met in Puntarenas, he said, "Ah, yes. We all came here with a girl we met in Puntarenas." Whatever that meant.

One night, Mac hopped onto the stool beside me, checked to make sure my recorder was on, and said to Allen and me, "I met a serial killer in Florida this winter."

"How's that?" Allen asked.

"Working on the crime documentary," Mac said. "We flew over to Florida to interview Danny Rolling, The Gainesville Ripper. We walked in there with the camera crew and he stood in this big empty room, handcuffed and in a jumpsuit—bunch of guards behind him. They'd painted a white line across the floor. They told us not to cross that line, but I walked right up to it, stuck my hand out, shook Danny's hand, and said, 'How's it goin' man? I'm Mac.'"

Allen didn't laugh at all, and began to wipe the bar.

I only chuckled because I figured I ought to, but I didn't like the pride in Mac's voice. "Why would you shake his hand?"

Mac pulled off his sunglasses and wiped a tear from his eye. "What do you mean?"

"Why did you cross the line and shake his hand?"

"'Cause that's what you do when you meet somebody."

"You wanted to show a serial killer respect?"

He shrugged and slipped his sunglasses back on. "That's right. I did."

"Serial killers aren't rebels."

Allen dropped his dirty rag in front of us, and put his hands on the bar. "Alright. How about we change the subject, boys? It's a family establishment."

"There's nobody here," Mac said.

"Don't matter," Allen said. "High season's around the corner. We gotta get into some nicer habits."

•

Every morning, while Mac slept off his hangover, I fought mine off—getting stoned and drinking coffee and writing about the farm. My best work came in the mornings, sometimes rising before the roosters to scribble notes in the manuscript's margins and re-writing paragraphs on the backs of pages.

What a joy it was to sway in a hammock while listening to my old recordings of the farm—to hear the tractor's engine and the men working—and know I was free. Some mornings, I'd find recordings of forgotten conversations with Mac from the night before—Mac saying things like, "If Adam and Eve were the first humans, then their kids slept with each other... so, is that how we became monkeys?" Or me asking, "Are you sure you want to be tripping out when you're seventy...in a spacesuit?"

•

After a few weeks, my farm chapter was complete. For days, I sat in an internet café and typed up the 5000-word chapter. I printed the ten pages for two dollars.

When I came home to celebrate the completed draft of *Curriculum Vitae*, Mac waddled out of the washroom in his worn-out briefs. He came over to me while I was smoking a bowl on the porch. His face looked pale. He was clasping his thigh.

I leaned back. "What are you doing?"

"Look. It's a tick."

The black bug had buried half its body into Mac's flesh.

He pinched his skin around the tick like the thing might burrow inside if he let go. "Burn it. It's the only way it'll come out."

I flicked the lighter. "Okay, stay still." I touched the tick, but it didn't move, so I held the flame closer, singeing Mac's hair. When I put the flame right on the bug, it still didn't move. "It's not going anywhere." I tapped the tick with the lighter. Its rear end fell off, but the head stayed inside. "Shit. It's not supposed to do that."

Mac snatched the wine bottle, limped back to the washroom, and muttered, "I'll cut it out."

The next morning, I slept in, dreaming I climbed a spiralling metal staircase outside the CN Tower at night. The rain poured, cold and red, and I slipped on the wet stairs, crawling on all fours and clutching the frozen steel in the howling wind. At the top, glass doors opened to a candle-lit room with red carpets. The room overlooked the Toronto skyline. At the back was a baby grand piano with a tiny wooden casket on top. Inside, I found my dead father—a miniature version of him only two feet tall. I touched the stubble on his cold, little chin and turned to find my tiny mother in another undersized casket—this one floating on a bed of white lilies. Her eyes were closed, but she was coughing and choking like an old rooster.

I opened my eyes. A rooster was going off outside my window. I found a chicken beside the hammock, calm and motionless in the sunlight, watching me. When I sat in the hammock, the chicken scampered into the living room, but then Mac charged from the house, swinging the broom like a lumberjack. Actually, I didn't immediately recognize him because he had shaved his head bald.

I lay back in the hammock.

Mac swatted over and over, but missed the chicken. Clumps of his hair clung to his sweaty back. Dried blood had splattered over his white scalp. He snapped the broom on the table leg. A half-empty wine bottle fell over and spilled to the floor. The chicken got away, but the rooster chased it around the yard, leapt onto its rump, tore into its feathers with its talons, and humped it.

"Why did you shave your head?" I asked.

He breathed heavily. "Looking for ticks." He grabbed my notepad off the table and carried it into the kitchen, and I hoped he wouldn't understand my handwriting enough to read anything I'd written about him. "Beer?" he asked as he headed back to the kitchen.

"No, thanks." I sat at the table and lit a joint.

Then he came out to the porch, beer in hand, and sat in the hammock and read more. But soon after, he held a hand over his right eye, to help him focus.

"Are you drunk already?" I asked.

"*Already*? I've been up all night shoveling a snowbank—I'm out of my goddamned skull." He scanned my pages and read, as a drop of blood ran over his ear. *I visited my father in the hospital and stood at the door watching him lying on his side with his back to me while my grandmother rubbed his back. He was crying like a baby... When he saw me later, he just winked—that was the closest we would ever come to talking about his death.* "Pffft! Where's the anger? All this slushy crap about your dad."

The cynical bastard. "You know your head's bleeding?"

He didn't hear me again. He found an empty page in my notepad and doodled. "I keep having this dream. This short shadow thing chases me through the city at night. It runs on its hands—when it catches me it jumps into my body, and I wake up."

He tossed the notepad to me. Its pages fluttered like bat wings. He'd drawn a dark, scratchy figure that walked on its hands. It looked like the rabid art of a possessed child—a thing to call a priest about. All of a sudden, I needed to know how the pills had twisted him, to see what life looked like through his big pupils.

The same chicken hopped onto the porch. Mac snatched his broken broom handle, chased it back down to the yard, and shouted, "These fucking rats!"

When he turned away, I snatched one of his pill bottles. I tried to open it fast, but he caught me and squawked, "What the hell ya doin'? Don't fuck around! I need those."

His eyes were begging me.

I slid the bottle across the table. "Just checking what's in here."

He didn't know I had two pills hidden in my hand—one red and one white. He clutched a bottle, popped the lid, and swallowed a pill. "These things stop me from losing my shit... After my mom died, I got hammered one night and lost it. I called my dad and told him I was going to off myself. He called the cops. They drove over to check on me and asked if I wanted to 'hurt' myself. I told 'em I was fine, but I only had the door open a crack—I guess they couldn't see the noose hanging in the hallway."

I wanted to say something about his mother—something in the way of condolence—but I felt awkward, like I was at a funeral. So, I laughed—smothering that sort of talk like one would smother a bomb.

That night in my bed, I remembered my mother telling me there was nothing the doctors could do for my father, that he would die. I remembered her calling my name as I ran to my bedroom. After a week in our local hospital, my father tore his IV out of his arm and insisted that the doctors and nurses let him go home. As he lay in a hospital bed in our living room, cared for by a nurse at night, I watched him wilt into a skeleton out of its mind on morphine. He never spoke of his death. And I avoided him just as much as he avoided the topic. Some nights, I would sit in the kitchen, eating a bowl of cereal, and look over at him, hearing his troubled breathing, and beg for any sort of magic to cure him. One morning, my mother walked into my room and told me he was dead. I hugged her, and she asked if I wanted to see him and say goodbye, and I said no.

I wondered if Mac's mother had said anything to him before she let go—things my father never bothered to say—things like 'I love you' and 'Goodbye.' Things to hold on to.

•

For Mac and me in Costa Rica, Christmas didn't exist, aside from one of us finding an old TV antenna with an extension cord dangling from its arms and then leaning it against the wall on the porch, and a neighbour agreeing it looked like a Christmas tree. I didn't like the antenna because it made me think of my family back home—uncles and aunts and cousins eating together and opening presents at midnight. I was grateful not to be there. The conversations had become awkward since my father died. The last Christmas we had with him, he weighed a hundred and ten pounds, and my aunt had bought him a pair of jeans—several sizes smaller than his usual—that she thought would fit him now. I remember thinking, Why would you buy a dying man new jeans? And later, around the dinner table, she had us hold hands while she prayed, even though our family had never been religious. My father, standing in his baggy new jeans as we awkwardly held hands, looked at me and rolled his eyes. Ten weeks later, he was dead.

•

On New Year's Eve, I went to withdraw money at the ATM in Cóbano. I thought there'd be seven or eight hundred dollars left in my account, but there was only a hundred and twenty.

An hour earlier, I had swallowed the pills I'd swiped from Mac, having saved them for such an occasion as New Year's Eve. Now they were hitting me hard. I sleepwalked out of the store and stood by the road, waiting for traffic to pass. I yawned over and over, tears running down my face. I thought I was dreaming. A mother and her little girl stood beside me. When a car went by, I took a step forward and the girl followed me. I stopped abruptly when I spotted another car coming, but the girl didn't notice. Her mother had to yank her back just in time. For a moment, I fell asleep with my eyes open. I watched the sun sail through the trees like a burning hot-air balloon, and searched for an explanation as to where my money had gone. Some time ago, I had formulated a belief that I could avoid a negative relationship with money by never looking at my balance. Now I was questioning that belief.

•

I went back to the house and slept a while. Then, with the strange numbness of Mac's pills still cloaking me, I drank beer and got stoned in the hammock. Close to midnight, I ran into Milla and Mac buying chicken skewers from a vendor. They were arguing about a story he'd written. He had shown it—the first story he'd ever written—to me two days earlier: It was about a wormy tendril that grew out of his penis and burrowed its way through Milla's body, through her skull, and into her brain, and then paralyzed and eventually killed her by feasting on her nervous tissue. It was hard to believe he'd let her read it.

"He wants to kill me," Milla said.

"Keep writing, Mac," I said. "Let all that craziness out of you."

Milla spat a chunk of chicken fat onto the road. "What kind of sick asshole writes crazy shit like that?"

"Sick asshole?" Mac objected. "Slim, two days ago, I woke up to this nutjob sitting on my chest, scratching my throat with a fucking nail file."

Milla pointed and almost stuck her finger in Mac's eyeball. "I didn't *scratch* you, you son of a bitch!"

Then Milla argued with a group of Italian guys. The argument escalated, and Milla shoved her chicken skewer in my hands and yelled at one of the guys, "What did you call me?" She clawed at his face and screeched some words that must have been Finnish. The guy grabbed her wrists and shouted, "Get this stupid bitch off me!" She struggled to free herself. Mac pulled the guy from behind and they all fell onto the road together. The guy's friends moved in and tried to pull their friend away from Milla, but she held onto the hood of his jacket, and then Mac began to smash his face with lefts and rights, like he couldn't decide which hand to use. All of this happened in the time it took me to steal a bite of Milla's chicken. I stepped toward the pile to pull them apart, and someone clocked my left eye.

I stumbled back and choked on the chicken. I bent over, clutching the skewer, coughing and spitting—no idea who had hit me.

"*¡Policía! ¡Policía!*" someone shouted.

The guys scattered.

Mac tried to take the chicken vendor's knife, but the vendor hid it from him and shouted, "No!" Then Mac took off after the Italians, but they were long gone.

"You okay?" Milla asked me. "Your eye."

"It's nothing," I said. "I think he missed me."

Milla skipped down the road back toward the hotel. Mac followed. There was something reckless about the way he walked, like someone looking for trouble. I stayed behind and watched them get smaller and smaller. Mac never looked back.

On my way home, I walked along the beach. My face pounded, and ceaseless shivering overtook me. I sped up to get warm, and ran past a group of young people dancing around a bonfire and shouting, "*¡Feliz año nuevo!*"

When I made it to the house, I slammed the gate shut. A gecko had tried to squeeze through the latch, and I'd accidentally squashed it. It fell to the ground, twitched in protest, and died. I held it up by its tail. Its guts had ruptured out of its stomach. I flung the thing in the bushes and ran up the stairs.

In the hammock, I slipped into my sleeping bag, hoping to warm up enough to stop my body from shaking. A tremendous panic came over me when I thought the squealing beach voices were coming closer. I felt the hammock rock, but it was motionless. A moment later, my heart pounded—so hard I could hear it outside my chest. I closed my eyes and tried to calm myself with slow breaths, but accepted that at any moment, I would hear the sound of my heart tearing itself open, and I would die.

Then a woman's voice whispered, "Dave."

I got startled. "Who's there?"

Nobody.

I walked into the kitchen in search of a beer, but the fridge was empty. On the counter streamed a trail of tiny ants. Hundreds of them poured in from the window. I followed them across the floor to our garbage can. I kicked the can away, exposing a horde of ants that scurried in every direction. Disgusted, I stomped on the ants and continued until I'd flattened them all. I looked to the counter again, to the ants ignorant of the slaughter below. I leaned in and squashed one with my finger. The ants scattered, running haphazardly, devastated and traumatized. I imagined their screams. Guilt overwhelmed me so much that I squashed every ant I could find, to liberate them from the fear I'd caused. I became fixated on the extermination, tapping my finger on the counter, over and over, killing fifty, sixty, a hundred ants before I tore myself away, ran to bed, and buried myself under the blankets.

When I closed my eyes, I saw red. Then I saw ants—hundreds of them squirming out of a slit in the dark, tearing it apart with gangly black legs, writhing out of the rotten opening, their frenzied legs growing into eyelashes around the hole—now a hollowed-out eye. I promised myself, if I could just get through the night, if I could just feel sober, I would never get high again. Because over the last seven years, there had been frequent visits to doctors for partial seizures, panic attacks, cold sweats, weight loss, rashes, sore kidneys, heart palpitations, or fears of colitis, phlebitis, syphilis, heart attacks, and strokes. There were senseless, paranoid concerns that I was cardio-dextrous, schizophrenic, or that perhaps a South-American parasite had flushed itself into the septic tank of my mind. So, over and over again, I promised to quit torturing myself.

I promised myself sobriety.

•

In the morning, I sat on the porch drinking water, just happy to be alive. I decided to hitchhike north—stick to the Pacific Coast, sleep in my tent along the beaches, and only spend money on food until I found

Ignacio's farm in Mexico. With a name like Hernandez-Hernandez, I figured he wouldn't be too hard to find. There, I would stay sober and finish polishing my book for Bella Chevalier. I had less than two months.

I rolled up *Curriculum Vitae* in a sweater and buried it in my backpack.

With everything packed, I was eating eggs on the porch when Mac stumbled into the yard, cranked out of his skull. He dropped into a chair. "You missed a crazy party. Flea was there."

"Flea?"

"Bass player for the Chili Peppers. I shook his hand and said, 'Hey man, I'm Mac. You want some blow?' Shit, he looked at me like I was a tapeworm." Mac laughed by himself.

"*Are* you?" I asked.

"Am I what, a tapeworm?" He snickered and pointed at my black eye. "What happened to you?"

"*What happened*? Did you forget ten Italian meatheads jumping me thanks to your crack pipe of a girlfriend?"

He chuckled. "Oh yeah, her ex and his surfer gang."

"I'm leaving today—going to Mexico. You know, you could have really gotten your shit together down here."

Mac stumbled back into the hammock and closed his eyes. "And what? Do *yoga*?"

I went into my room and stuffed my things into my backpack, and when I came out, Mac was asleep, so I just walked away.

When we were eighteen, Mac and I had left a bar in Ottawa after closing time. We came across a rig stopped at a red light, and hopped on the back of the trailer, holding on to the doors. I jumped off by the time the truck had crossed the intersection, but as the truck sped up, it was too late for Mac to jump. And when the traffic light ahead turned green, the truck sped up even more, and then Mac was gone, up the on-ramp for Highway 17 in the middle of winter.

And here I was, walking through the rain forest seven years later, still feeling the way I did, standing alone on that snow-covered road and waiting for Mac to die. And as I lugged my backpack farther up the road, what popped into my head was the sight of him back on the porch, hanging from his neck.

So, I turned in to Las Olas, which was closed, and left a note under one of the barstools that was flipped upside-down on the bar; I was hoping Allen would find it.

Mac has talked about offing himself. He tied a noose. Don't let him die.

CHAPTER SEVEN

I hitched a ride in a pickup to a shipyard in Jacó, where the rain was falling hard and loud. I chatted with a couple of workers in hard hats, who said I might have a chance of hopping on a Filipino ship bound for Mazatlán, leaving in three days. They pointed me to their cranky boss: a tall, fat man with a high-pitched voice and a big, black moustache like a push broom. At first, he walked by me, ignoring the white boy standing in his shipyard with a black eye, but when I spoke Spanish to him and apologized for the disturbance, he came over.

Rain dripped off our noses.

"Where you from?" he asked.

"Canada. I'm out of money—making my way to Mexico. I heard you can help me find a ride on a Filipino ship."

I followed the man, and we found shelter under an awning. He grumbled, "You'd have to ask the captain."

"Great. Is there somewhere around here I could pitch my tent?"

"You want to sleep outside? For three days?"

"I don't have a choice. I'm broke."

The look in his eyes had changed. "Listen, kid. Don't get on that ship."

"Why not?"

"You don't want to be stuck on that ship."

What did he know about the Filipino crew? What were they shipping? I imagined floating over the Pacific. No land on the horizon. No escape. I'd be locked in the engine room, shoveling coal—if that was what a ship ran on—but whatever it was, I'd be the one shoveling it.

"Fine," I said. "I'll hitchhike."

"Hitchhike? Have you not heard of the Mara Salvatrucha?" he said. "It's a gang. They'll make you look much worse than you do now, with your black eye. Can't you call your family for help?"

I shook my head.

•

With my shoes sopping wet, I rode the shipyard workers' bus to the Puntarenas bus station. There, I found a bus idling, with a sign in the front window that read: *Peñas Blancas-Nicaragua Frontera*—the Nicaraguan border. I approached the driver as he closed the cargo doors.

"*Esta lleno*," he said. "There's another bus tomorrow."

"I have no money. Can I sit on your stairs? I'd have to hitchhike. I hear there are gangs."

He agreed to let me ride in the aisle for free.

Inside the bus packed with tourists, I set my backpack down, sat on it, and changed my wet, stinky socks. I rode for two hours on the muggy bus, and plotted my journey to Mazatlán while eating all six of my *guayaba* cookies.

•

At the Peñas Blancas border, I walked forward. The lot was crawling with hot cars lined up in the late afternoon sun, waiting to cross the border, and I knew

I'd eventually find a lift. For now, anything to take me farther north would do.

When I entered Nicaragua, vendors called after me to buy candies, buses tempted me with air-conditioning, and a row of rigs waited in a line. One of the truckers was a man with a fresh haircut and a baby face.

"*¿Desculpe, vas hacia el Norte?*" I shouted over his rumbling engine.

He tipped his sunglasses down to take a look at me. He looked around, seemed content no one was watching us, then offered a discreet nod.

I ran to the passenger side with a big smile, because for the first time in my life, I was climbing into a rig.

The driver was a Honduran named Rufino. We roasted in the cab together and waited for traffic to move. Photos of his wife and three young children were taped to his dashboard, and a blue rosary was wrapped around his gear shift.

"*¿De donde eres?*" he asked.

"Canada."

"Why do you speak Spanish?"

"French is my first language. They're similar."

"They are?"

A group of children ran after us and shouted for money. Rufino tossed change out the window. Outside my door, another group ran alongside the truck, dragging their shoeless feet in the dirt. I found a few *colones* from my bag and flung it at them. The kids screeched and scurried after the coins. They looked up at me as if I were riding a parade float, and they cried for more, but I rolled the window up and tried to ignore them.

"Roll it down," Rufino said. "It's too hot."

I rolled down the window and the children shouted at me. I couldn't handle their desperate faces. I scooped the rest of my *colones* from my bag and hurled them through the air.

When we took off, a merciful breeze filled the cab. In the hills, we passed two more children on the side of the road. One of them held up a large, dead iguana. Rufino saw the look on my face and said, "They're selling roadkill. *A comer*." He chuckled at my disgusted expression.

"*¿A donde vas?*" he asked.

"Mexico."

"I'm heading to the Honduran border tonight," he said. "But I'm going around the lake and up the mountains. It might be better for you if I drop you off outside Managua in a couple of hours—more traffic in Managua. You can get to El Salvador faster from there, through León."

"How far is the Honduran border?"

"Around seven hours, but the border will be closed. Makes no sense for you to go that way instead of straight north."

Because I had yet to see a map, I had no idea what he meant, but I knew if he dropped me off in a city at night, I'd have to pay for a room. I figured I'd stick with Rufino. At least in the mountains, I could sleep in my tent anywhere and start fresh at sunrise.

•

That night, Rufino stopped at a restaurant and I bought us *gallo pinto* with eggs.

"You're brave to be hitchhiking," he said.

"I'm not brave. I just don't have a choice."

"Still, I wish I could travel like you."

"Do it," I said. "Quit your job and travel."

He shook his head. "*No puedo*."

I remembered the photos of his family on his dashboard.

"You're really hitchhiking to Mexico?" he asked.

"Yeah, and to the U.S., eventually. I can get a job delivering a car to Canada from there."

"It's too far! Can your parents fly you home?"

I shook my head. "I don't want to go home. It's minus thirty up there."

Rufino stopped eating. "I don't understand what minus thirty means—what does that even feel like?"

"Your nostril hairs freeze together, and your truck doesn't start, unless you plug it in."

"You plug your cars?"

•

At night, the truck's headlights illuminated the narrow mountain road. We hardly spoke. Rufino's hands squeezed the wheel. Down in the forest valley, a village's tiny lights flickered, nestled and forgotten in the belly of the Earth. When we reached the clouds, we could no longer see where the cliffs ended and the empty space began, and we rubbernecked our heads toward the windshield, in search of the road. What would it sound like if we slid off the mountain and rolled over and over into the unseen chasm? How long before we tasted blood and my little universe turned black?

Around 10 p.m., we stopped behind a lengthy row of rigs and cars parked along the mountainside.

"*¿Un accidente?*" I asked.

"This is the border. They're all waiting for it to open tomorrow." He turned the engine off, and the mountain silence took over. "There's no room for you to sleep in the truck. But ask the vendors for a room; they'll rent you one."

I shook his hand and thanked him several times before stepping out of the truck and into the night, where I looked for a place to pitch my tent along the road. Drivers slept in their vehicles as I walked past. Around the bend was the border—nothing more than a gloomy wooden shack and a simple barricade. Up ahead, a generator droned. I approached two ramshackle restaurants and a vendor stand set up on the dirt road under tarps and hanging work lights that illuminated the drizzling rain.

A woman wiped dusty plastic tables under a tarped roof. She wore a white wool sweater and had big, sleepy eyes—looked to be in her late twenties. She smiled at me when I approached. Beside her, three young children sat in the dirt, torturing an injured dung beetle.

"*Buenas noches*," I said. "Is there anywhere I can camp for the night? I have no money for a room."

She glanced over her shoulder, to a group of loud men who played cards and drank beer. "*Sí*. You can sleep in the back," she whispered, before leading me through the dark, to a path between the restaurant and a little house.

We approached an eight-by-eight wooden shed, empty and damp with a dirt floor and no light.

"It's quiet here," she said and walked away.

I stepped into the shack and unrolled my sleeping bag on the ground. I pulled my ridiculous steak knife out and slid it into my bag, ready to stab at whatever critter came along. Moments later, someone tapped on the door.

"¿Sí?"

The woman entered and handed me an old piece of foam to sleep on. She lit a votive candle and placed it next to my bag, illuminating the rough, wood-slatted shed.

"Where are you from?" she asked.

"Canada."

"So far. I've never gone very far." The longing in her voice was shattered by thunderous laughter from next door. Her expression became worried, and she turned away. One of the men at the card table must have trapped her on this mountain, like a mudslide.

•

Roosters screamed.

I woke in the gloomy shack, bundled up with my bag over my head and shouting, "What's my name? What's my name?" Then, as truck engines roared and headlights beamed through the wall slats, I woke from that terrifying dream. And my life came back to me: I was on a dirt floor in the middle of nowhere.

After crossing the border, I hitched a ride in a hatchback. The driver was Luis, a Spanish teacher with glasses and black, shoulder-length hair pulled behind his ears. He asked a lot of questions.

"What happened to your eye?" he asked.

"I got hit by a surfboard."

"How is it you ran out of money?"

"I guess I lost track."

"Why Mexico?"

"To write," I said.

"How serendipitous! I'm a writer too—a poet."

I reached in the backseat, dug my hand into my backpack, and pulled out my manuscript. At the sight of the rolled-up novella, Luis smiled and said, "You know what, I'll drive you to the bus station in Tegucigalpa."

"You don't have to if it's out of your way."

"Don't worry about it," he said. "I appreciate the company of a fellow writer. We'll talk shop!"

Luis talked all the way to Tegucigalpa, and when we got there, we bought sandwiches. I didn't want to hitchhike from the city, so I bought the cheapest ticket to San Salvador.

We ate our ham-and-cheese sandwiches at a table outside the station and watched buses come and go in the brown, dusty lot.

Luis stirred his coffee. "Why do you write?"

"I don't know. Why do you?"

He lowered his cup. "I write to connect with people. Our work should stir emotions in others, if it's art." At the blank look on my face, Luis asked, "Do you follow me? Do I speak too fast?"

"I understand," I said. "I just don't write to connect with anyone."

"A writer must feel his audience—feel the camera and microphone aimed at his chest—to hear the groans, and sighs, but above all to hear the applause."

"Forget the applause," I said. "I'd rather write anonymously."

He laughed. "How long have you felt like that—like an introvert?"

I didn't want to tell Luis about how I became an introvert.

I was twelve, and my best friend died in a car crash with his parents. My father took me to the wake—to the endless bouquets and haunting photos of my friend and his dead parents and the traumatized school kids in their best clothes and everyone sobbing over closed caskets. That night, recalling the last memory I had of my friend—where he'd karate-chopped me in the throat over some argument about a girl, I went into my parents' room and cried. My mother hugged me. My father left the room, and my mother said, "Kiddo, you'll have to stop crying or we'll send you to a shrink." I stopped crying and went back to bed. After that night, I never let my parents see me cry, not even at my father's wake, when I stood over his casket and stared at his eyelids and lips, wondering if they'd been sewn or glued shut. Later, kissing his forehead at my mother's suggestion, I felt the hard coldness of his empty body and understood he was gone. I didn't even cry in the reception room where my family was crying. I found an empty seat next to two men I didn't know—probably guys who worked at the mine with my father. They must not have known who I was, because when talking about my father, one of them said to the other, "I don't even recognize him in that coffin. Hard to believe that was a two-hundred-pound man."

Anyway, I didn't want to tell Luis about any of that stuff.

"I think of writing as my instrument, you see?" Luis began.

I stopped listening, distracted by a boy, about fifteen, who had entered the yard. He carried a bucket and a sponge, and he pulled a hose along as he hobbled and dragged his rubber boots—the toes of which pointed inward. An elderly man in the yard caught me gawking at the boy. He waved to get my attention as he snuck up behind the kid, who kneeled to scrub a bus tire. The elderly man stepped on the boy's boots and flattened them to the ground. The boy had no feet. The elderly man laughed at my stunned expression.

"You see that?" I said. "That's the stuff I write about."

•

In a crowd outside a rusty bus, I overheard three men making cracks about my yellowing black eye. Each of them carried their belongings in a plastic grocery bag and they sat close to me inside the bus. The bigger one in the group leaned over. "America! You go Chicago?"

"*Hablo Español*," I said.

He looked back to his friends and shrugged.

I gave him the spiel—told him I was broke and heading for Mexico. And I made sure to tell him all of that in Spanish to discourage them from robbing me.

We chatted for a while and pretty soon, I trusted them. They planned to swim across the Cuilco River into Mexico, hop a train, and ride it to the U.S. border. They talked about a *coyote* in Northern Mexico who would smuggle them into the U.S., so they could work eight-dollar-an-hour construction jobs that Edwin's cousin had lined up for them in Chicago. Edwin was the group's leader. He wore his grandmother's white cardigan, which was so small, it only covered half his back. "She gave me this to remember her because she thinks she'll never see me again."

From San Salvador, I hitchhiked with the guys all day through Santa Lucia, Santa Ana, and Ahuachapán. I secretly recorded their conversations and took notes as they negotiated rides with drivers and haggled food prices with vendors who fed us *pupusas* and fish soups.

•

In the evening, we entered Guatemala, and three young men in a hatchback picked us up. They let the four of us cram into the backseat and took us into the town of Valle Nuevo. I was filled with optimism. Two days on the road, and I was already halfway to Mazatlán.

The police pulled us over immediately.

Two scrawny officers approached the car. I felt safely hidden between two Hondurans, my backpack laid across our laps. It wasn't me they were after. Edwin knew right away what they wanted. He stepped out, and their muffled conversation was cordial and reminiscent of a drug deal. Edwin handed the officers a few bills, and they let us on our way.

•

We were dropped off somewhere outside Valle Nuevo. There were no streetlights along the darkened road into the suburbs—just the smell of burning garbage and the sounds of barking dogs.

A man approached us. He wore a cowboy hat and boots. His name was Gilberto. Their conversation moved so fast I could only make out that Gilberto was also a migrant, from Nicaragua, on his way to San Francisco in three days, and that we could spend the night with him.

Gilberto unlocked a padlock on the metal door of a tin-roof, cinder-block shack off the road. The door opened to a dark and dingy space with a concrete floor, furnished with nothing but a hammock.

I listened to the rapid slang in the darkness and followed none of it, for the most part. But I understood when Edwin spoke about the passage from Honduras to America: "My brother tried to make the trip on his own two years ago, but he got robbed in Veracruz by two cops. That scared the hell out of him—so he turned back."

Later, we lay on the hard floor by candlelight and used our sweaters for pillows. I left my sleeping bag in my backpack because no one else had one and I didn't want to make anyone jealous. I sprawled out on the floor in my shorts, with my hood pulled over my head, T-shirt draped over my legs, and shuddered at the thought of cops robbing me—losing my manuscript and every revision I'd made.

•

In the morning, we pooled our money and Gilberto took us to an outdoor restaurant, where we devoured a great breakfast of eggs, beans, goat cheese, and coffee. Across the street, a twelve- or thirteen-year-old boy yanked a chicken from its pen. He tied its feet with a string and hung the chicken on a post in the yard. The boy pinched feathers on the chicken's throat and tore them out. The chicken violently flapped its wings and began screeching. Holding a short machete at arm's length and looking away, the boy slashed at the chicken's throat. The chicken convulsed, slamming itself against the post and flapping its wings, trying to free itself. The cut was too shallow. The boy looked to his father, but he paid no attention to the boy, who then stepped toward the chicken and finally pulled the machete back and chopped at the neck. The knife sank into the post with a solemn, merciful thud. The chicken's head fell and landed softly into a small pile of old feathers.

After breakfast, we walked north toward a gas station, where we approached a man fuelling up his small, beat-up pickup. He said if we wanted to ride in the box, he could take us as far as Chimaltenango, outside Guatemala City.

I sat with my back to the cab, a shirt over my head to shade me from the sun, as we zipped along the Pan-American Highway into the mountains of the Sierra Madre. Everything went by under enormous skies—plantations, rivers, and villages with kids outside rickety houses, shoeless and in ragged clothes and diapers. There were roadside vendors selling pineapples, mangos, and papayas, and smoke billowing from firepits and garbage heaps, as the green hills rose to form mountains or maybe volcanoes, before descending into the smog and traffic of Guatemala City.

•

Outside Chimaltenango, we jumped from the truck and entered a *tienda*, where we pooled our money once again and bought bread, cheese, bananas, and water. I asked the little girl behind the counter if I could use their washroom. The girl stepped outside the store and hollered a few words up the street. Seconds later her younger sister, about ten years old, approached the store, dragging her little flip-flops through the dirt. The girl took my hand and escorted me back to their house.

I followed her through a metal door in a concrete wall that opened to a little courtyard with a kitchen under a corrugated plastic roof, where *caldo de pollo* simmered in a giant pot. The girl spoke like an adult as she scuttled to the kitchen. "Go ahead and use the washroom inside. I have to check the soup."

After using the washroom in the dark, musky house, I crossed the small living area with two sofas at one end, and a queen-sized bed at the other. Sunlight beamed through cracks in the closed blinds, and something moved on the bed. It was a baby, staring at the ceiling with a big smile on its face.

"*Hola*," I whispered as I stepped toward it. "Why are you all alone?"

A movement against the wall startled me. It was a tiny woman. She stood with her hands behind her back.

"*Hola*," I said. "Didn't see you there. Is that your baby?"

She stepped into the sunlight, smiling. She was just a child.

"*Hola*," I said, again.

"Hiss my brroder."

"Oh, how old is he?"

She shrugged. "*No se.*"

"Where are your parents?"

"They work."

"David!" Edwin shouted from outside. "We have a ride!"

"I have to go," I said, but didn't move. I couldn't believe these children—who changed diapers, cooked soup, ran a corner store—had welcomed a strange man into their home.

"*Adiós*," she said, with such sincerity that it broke my heart. I handed the girl twenty *quetzales*. "For you and your sisters."

Outside, Edwin and the guys spoke with another man in a beat-up pickup truck. "He can give us a ride to El Carmen!"

•

In El Carmen, we paid for a single room. We'd arrived at the Mexican border. They would leave me tomorrow, off to find the Cuilco River and then to

Tapachula, where they'd hop on their train, and who knew what would happen after that.

We let Edwin have the bed, and the rest of us sat on the floor and drank beer. I had bought a six-pack to thank them for leading me this far. As we slouched and sipped, Edwin said, "I'm ashamed to tell you, David, but when we first met you on the bus, I thought of robbing you."

I laughed. "I know."

•

The guys walked with me toward the border the next day, down a street crowded with pedestrians and taxis—a dead end, for them. They would soon be knee-deep in muddy riverbanks. They hugged me and patted me on the back and wished me luck, as they stood there with nothing but their plastic bags. I decided they wouldn't make it. They'd be arrested, or else fall off a train and die. I dropped my bag and pulled out my grey hoodie and handed it to Edwin. "You want this?"

"*¡Claro! ¡Gracias!*" He hugged me again.

"I wish you'd just go home and give your grandmother back her cardigan," I said. "But I guess it's too stretched out now, anyway."

He smiled. "*Sí*, David. It's too far gone."

CHAPTER EIGHT

Moments after entering Mexico, I crossed an intersection and a car behind me made a right turn onto the narrow street, but had to stop because a rusty, local bus was wedged between parked cars and took up most of the street. The vehicles now faced each other head-on, both drivers honking their horns as if whoever could honk the longest would force the other to move. I stopped to watch how this would unfold—how long would it take before the car driver backed up, realizing it was much easier and logical for him to do so than the bus. After a minute of arguing with bus the driver's assistant, the car driver bashed his horn again and wouldn't let go. The bus driver's assistant hopped out of the open door, approached the car driver's door, and through his open window, walloped him with five or six lefts. No longer comfortable being a witness, I turned away and carried on.

•

Outside Tuxtla Chico, I scored a series of rides in *combis* through Tapachula, Feliciano Renauld, and Los Toritos. Sometimes they crammed ten of us in the vans, and on every ride, some local wanted to talk with me. I loved to small-talk in the more familiar Mexican Spanish. *"¿De donde eres, güero?"* they'd ask. And, *"¿Donde aprendiste Español?"* they needed to know.

When we stopped to pick up passengers outside Los Toritos, I stepped out to buy a ham-and-cheese sandwich. A white man approached. He had a scruffy, grey beard, ratty hair, dirty jeans, a torn T-shirt, and carried a backpack one-quarter the size of mine—a school bag, really.

"Hey, man. Buy me a sandwich?" His unfriendly eyes weren't asking.

"I can't. I'm broke," I said.

He followed me into the *combi,* and they slid the door shut. Because the scruffy guy sat across from me on the sideways benches, he had to watch me eat. It did cross my mind to share half my sandwich with him, but he kept eyeballing me like he might just fight me over it, so I hurried and wolfed the whole thing.

"*¿Eres David?*" an old *campesino* asked me.

For a long time, he had sat quietly in the back, under his straw hat.

"*Sí,*" I said. "How did you know my name?"

He grinned under his grey moustache. "*¿Veniste de Costa Rica, verdad?*"

"How did you know that?"

The *campesino* chuckled.

We pulled over at a military checkpoint.

"*Señor*, how did you know my name?"

The *campesino* stepped out and walked away as the *Federales,* armed with machine guns, asked for our papers. I handed over my passport and watched the old *campesino* wander down the highway. But what could I do, chase after the *campesino* and demand to know why he knew things about me? The *Federales* handed back my passport, then asked for the scruffy guy's papers.

He launched a protest. "No need *passaporte*. I'm *Americano. Americano!*"

Three more agents came to the door and ordered him to step out. Outside, they surrounded the man, slid our door shut, and instructed our driver to move along. I couldn't make out the heated argument outside. As we slowly pulled away, everyone in the *combi* looked back—even the driver. The man tried to free himself, but the *Federales* slammed him to the ground.

I thought, maybe I really should have shared my sandwich with the guy.

We hit the road, and I turned to the pregnant woman who sat beside me.

"*Señora*, how did that *señor* know my name?"

"*Es un shaman.*"

"A shaman? Should I have followed him?"

She shrugged. "*No sé.*"

CHAPTER NINE

I bought a ticket for overnight bus rides to Acapulco, because with the heavy tourist traffic, I figured it would be a good place to hitch a ride to Mazatlán in the morning. I withdrew everything I could from an ATM. I had six hundred pesos left.

A young Mexican woman stood alone at the back of the bus, stuffing her backpack and a pair of bongos overhead. She wore a faded poncho, red and white and too big for her, with sleeves that dangled far below her hands. I took the seat in front of her. But just as I wanted to say something to her, a man's voice called out from the front of the bus, "Zuriaa?"

"Back here," she said.

A tall Mexican guy came down the aisle, lugging a big backpack and carrying a guitar. He looked about thirty and wore a white Gypsy shirt. His black hair, parted in the middle, drooped over his face—the long, bony face of the Aztecs.

His guitar was a black, thin-body, semi-acoustic. When he saw me looking at it, he said in a raspy voice, "*¿Hola. Hablas Español?*"

"*Sí*," I said.

"You play music?"

"*Sí.*"

"Can you play bongos? She can't hold a beat."

I nodded and felt embarrassed for the girl, but she didn't seem to mind.

"Where are you going?" he asked.

"Acapulco."

The way they looked at me, I knew they thought I was going to a resort.

"I'm hitchhiking from there to my friend's farm outside Mazatlán."

"That's too bad," he said. "You could have busked with us in Oaxaca City."

"*Sí*," the girl said, smiling with a mouthful of braces. "Come with us."

"I would, but I don't have any money."

"Neither do we," he said. "But we have weed."

I smiled.

"I'm Antonio. This is Zuriaa."

I shook hands with them.

"Busk with us in Oaxaca," Antonio said. "We split everything three ways."

I decided busking was the responsible thing to do. Ignacio would only feed and house me on his farm, so I'd need spending money. And with money, I'd be able to take a bus to Mazatlán instead. Besides, I was still dreading having to hitchhike from a city like Acapulco.

•

In the morning, I followed Antonio and Zuriaa through the cobbled streets of Oaxaca City. When we reached the *zócalo*, standing outside the *Palacio de Gobierno*, I remembered my first time in Oaxaca City. I was in an artisan shop on the second floor, when everything shook as if a gas truck had driven into the building. Pottery fell off the shelves, bursting and scattering across the tiles, and then a crack ripped through the concrete wall like a bolt of lightning. Then came the dizzy feeling of death as the 7.4 earthquake rattled on. Outside, a flock of birds fled from the trees. My consciousness escaped out the window, and I became one of the little grey birds, watching the earthquake tear chunks of concrete off buildings. It killed eighteen people.

•

We cut through a market with tables and heaps of clothes, toys, meats, fruits, and vegetables, all under tarps held up by wooden poles cemented into old buckets. From there, we crossed a pedestrian bridge into San Juanito, a quiet neighbourhood fifteen minutes outside of Oaxaca.

For fifty pesos a day, Antonio rented us an unfurnished room on the second floor of a dilapidated complex. The room smelled like bleach and sewage. Peeling green paint covered the concrete walls. A partial wall concealed a grimy toilet with no seat and no water. To flush it, we'd have to use an old bucket and a hose from the communal balcony, which overlooked a loud, busy courtyard weaved with clotheslines made of old rope and shoestrings. It was a place where dogs barked, children shouted, firecrackers popped, and the sad thud of a deflated soccer ball beat against a concrete wall.

I stuffed my six hundred pesos in a dirty sock at the bottom of my backpack, resolved not to spend it.

•

Later we walked back to the *zócalo* and sat at a plastic table on the sidewalk. A golden church rested in the background, with mountains in the hazy distance. An old lady sold food out the front door of her home. The smell of warm tortillas wafted out of her window.

Everyone in the neighborhood dropped by, talking to the old lady, to each other, and even to us, as though we were family. Antonio bought us three *memelas*—fat tortillas smeared with refried beans and goat cheese, hot sauce, and lime juice.

After lunch, Antonio picked his faded old bongos off the ground and handed them over.

"We'll play on the buses," he said. "We'll make enough for lunch and dinner. We play snappy songs, which gives us enough time to collect money before the passengers get off."

When a local bus came toward us, crawling through traffic, and coughing up black smoke, Antonio stood, and we followed him across the street, while he held his guitar in the air for the bus driver to see. The driver let us on for free.

"Does he know you?" I asked.

"No," he said. "He knows we're busking."

On the bus full of commuters, we stood in the aisle and leaned on the backrests. After he found space for himself and his guitar, Antonio strummed a three-chord Mexican pop song. I hunched over with the bongos between my legs and played along. The song was simple and repetitive and awfully cliché, and when Antonio belted out the corny lyrics, Zuriaa singing along off-key, I couldn't help but cringe and wonder why anybody would give us money. I wanted to disappear.

As the first song came to a merciful end, Zuriaa threaded her way down the aisle, asking passengers for change. Perhaps she charmed them with her innocent face, because they were handing over coins, which she dumped in the pocket of Antonio's backpack. During the second, equally boring song, she stood beside me, dumped a few more coins in the bag, and nudged me with her hip. "Move your body, *güero*."

"What?"

"Dance! You're so stiff."

"I'm not a dancer."

She giggled. "Wow, your face is red." She pulled out her disposable camera and took a photo of me.

•

We rode the next bus to the park, where Antonio found a guy to sell him a *tubo*—weed packaged in rolled-up newspaper, twisted at both ends like a Tootsie Roll.

Antonio rolled a joint, while Zuriaa counted the change in the pocket of Antonio's bag. "Thirty-five."

Antonio lit his joint and said, "David, you seemed unmotivated."

"I didn't know those songs," I said, worried they'd throw me out of the band already.

"You need motivation," he said, handing me the joint. "Those radio songs are easy money. That's why we play them on the bus. You'll be happy we played them when we're eating chicken and fresh tortillas and drinking beer."

We were stoned and sauntered back to the road. The life on the streets unfolded slowly now, as we passed every colour of Oaxacan life: young men sitting on curbs with nothing to do; old people pushing makeshift trolleys carrying crates of fruits; and a woman seated on a pink, plastic stool and breastfeeding on the sidewalk. Later, we stopped to watch an older man who mixed concrete with a shovel—just a pile of sand and cement on the street that he then splattered onto the broken stairs outside his home.

When we reached a busy street, Antonio stuck his guitar in the air for bus drivers to see. With weed, everything was fun. We hustled for two or three hours, hopping on and off buses, never straying too far from the *zócalo*, playing the same two songs every ten minutes for a new busload of ears. I stopped thinking about what we were playing, and just played. Nothing mattered but the music of Zuriaa dumping change into Antonio's bag.

As Antonio had promised, we sat in the *zócalo*, stuffing our faces with tacos for dinner. But there was no money left over for us to split three ways.

Antonio explained he'd been busking all over Northern Mexico, Guatemala, and Belize, for five years straight. "My ex thinks I'm a junkie addicted to travelling," he said. "Maybe she's right, but she doesn't know what it's like for me—to feel homesick, even when you're home."

I understood what he meant because I could never stay anywhere longer than three or four months—always bored, always desirous of something undefined, and of course, never finding it.

"We're staying here a few weeks," he said. "Then we head to Veracruz for *Carnaval*. I always make more money there." He turned to me then. "Maybe from there, we'll go up to San Luis Potosí and Real de Catorce—that would get you closer to your friend's farm, with money in your pocket."

I smiled and agreed to follow them to Veracruz, beginning to think that maybe I wouldn't have to work on Ignacio's farm after all—that I could finish *Curriculum Vitae* while on the road with Antonio, and could then write about our travels until Bella Chevalier sent back her notes.

•

In the evening, we walked back to our San Juanito room and sat on the red floor tiles, which were cracked and faded, like many things in San Juanito. We had bought two *caguamas*, which are one-litre bottles of beer.

Antonio stood by the wall, inspecting two wires that protruded from an open outlet box in the wall. He flicked the wires with his finger.

"Don't touch those!" Zuriaa shouted.

Antonio swiped a hand at her, fetched a little stereo from his backpack, then tried to hook its plug to the wires through the holes in the prongs. "I know what I'm doing." When he finally managed to hook both wires to the stereo plug, the stereo's red light came on. He hit Play, then picked up his guitar and played along to Manu Chao's *Merry Blues*. He pointed at a baseball-sized hole on the edge of his guitar's face. "My ex-wife did that. She picked up the heaviest rock she could lift and tried to squash my guitar."

"Not because of me," Zuriaa said.

I laughed and grabbed the recorder out of my bag. "You guys mind if I record you? I'm a writer."

"*¡Qué chido!*" Antonio shouted. "I noticed you're always in your notepad. You can write about everything that'll happen to us!"

Then on and on they went, reliving some story I couldn't quite piece together because of their Mexico City slang, but it had something to do with Antonio's wife leaving him, and Zuriaa picking up the pieces.

"David, *La Vibra* brought us together," he said. "All *viajeros* drift down the same path. That's like a universal law, you see. That's why I know Faustina will be in Veracruz and then Real de Catorce."

"Who's Faustina?" I asked.

"She's a traveller."

"Antonio was in love with her," Zuriaa said.

"Everybody's in love with her," he said.

•

After three weeks in Oaxaca, we hadn't made enough money to pocket anything—just enough to keep us fed, stoned, and drunk. I was okay with our idling, because we were sustaining ourselves and because every morning, before Antonio and Zuriaa woke, I made notes on my manuscript—now due in five weeks.

•

One morning, I washed on the balcony with the bucket and cold water from the garden hose. A brown dog, thin and weak-looking, chained day and night to the balcony railing, kept a vigilant eye on me.

"*Buenos días*," I said to the dog.

A woman stepped onto the balcony in her pyjamas. "He's not friendly," she said, as she began sweeping up some dried turds. The dog gnashed at her and began to bark. She yelped and jumped back, then jabbed the dog in the head with the butt end of her broom and shouted, "*¡Hijo de puta!*"

"*¡Señora!*" I yelled, my wet hair dripping. "Stop!"

Swiping hair from her flustered face, the woman composed herself. "My husband hates when it barks."

"You ever think to take it for a walk?"

She turned red, dropped her broom, and shrank down the hall like a child sent to her room.

•

That same morning, in the *zócalo*, Antonio went off in search of breakfast while Zuriaa and I sat in the shade under a tree. She spread a tie-dyed sheet on the ground and displayed her handmade jewellery. She hadn't sold a thing in Oaxaca, and I doubted she had ever sold anything, because her jewellery—beads, leather, twisted wires, and cheap stones—looked like the clumsy efforts of a child. And she was practically a child—only eighteen.

"Where did you meet Antonio?" I asked.

"On the Pacific," she said. "Just before we met you."

This surprised me. "You mean, you met a month ago?"

She nodded, taking the bongos from me and tapping them quietly with her fingers.

"Was his wife there?"

Without answering my question, and before she could find any sort of rhythm, Zuriaa let loose, thumping and thrashing the skins senselessly.

I squirmed when I noticed the many pedestrians observing us. People were pointing at her and laughing.

"Are you being serious?" I asked.

She smiled and carried on, moving her body stupidly. "About what? Are you embarrassed?"

"No," I said, even though I was. "Listen. Listen! I saw a woman beat a little dog."

"What?"

"With a broom! On the balcony! Can you stop playing? They keep the dog chained there!"

She finally stopped battering the poor bongos. "You love dogs?"

"No. Are you listening?"

She wasn't listening, because some guy had shouted her name from across the *zócalo*. Zuriaa ran to him just as Antonio returned with *tamales*.

"*¡Chingao!*" Antonio muttered. "That's Púas, her ex."

Antonio stood and took his guitar. "I'm taking my *lyra* for repairs."

I'd never heard anybody call a guitar a *lyra* before.

•

Back in the room, Antonio strummed a pink classical guitar—a loaner from the repair shop—while Púas and Zuriaa sat on her sleeping bag together. Púas was a handsome guy in his early twenties, clean-cut, wiry build—better-looking than Antonio. Ever since they'd met in the *zócalo*, Zuriaa had not left Púas' side. She sorted through a bag of jewellery parts he had brought for her. He had come from their hometown of Toluca to find her, and told me he had recently applied for a Canadian work visa. Antonio kept a sideways eye on them. As far as I could tell, he had simply been a placeholder for Púas, and now he was like me—just another guy in the room.

Someone knocked on our door. In walked a stocky Mexican man with a face like a cinder block. He wore a wrinkled, grey suit and spoke in a gruff voice. "Hello, Antonio. You remember me?"

"Of course, I do." Antonio introduced us to Miguel, who lived in the complex.

Zuriaa rolled up Púas' bag for Miguel to sit on.

Antonio said, "Zuriaa, do we have any change for a *caguama*?"

I'd never seen Zuriaa carry money, but she patted her pockets, perhaps pretending to search for change.

Miguel put up his hand. "It's on me."

•

Hours later, a drunken Miguel had his jacket off, tie loosened, and shirt unbuttoned. His type had clung to us before—the ones tethered and desperate to travel, but too fearful to move. But every stranger, like Miguel, had been welcome to indulge in our amusement, music, and stories.

After he'd taken a couple of hits off a joint, Miguel wouldn't stop talking—and, we assumed, lying. "I know what it's like on the road," he said. "I'll have to hit the ol' highway again for work next week."

"What type of work?" Zuriaa asked.

"Anthropology."

Zuriaa lit up. "Hey! That's what my parents wanted me to study."

Miguel sighed. "I'm not sure you would have been up for it, sweetheart. It's hard work—a lot of travel involved."

Zuriaa replied, "I camped on the Pacific for a week, and we hitchhiked here. And we're going to Veracruz and then Real de Catorce, so..."

Miguel snorted and looked to the rest of us for support. He found none. "You'd never make it. I've hitchhiked across the States and all over Mexico for my work, you know."

I knew he was lying, but I didn't bother to say anything, because everyone seemed content to let him ramble on since he'd gone out for more beer. Zuriaa pointed to the joint Miguel had stopped smoking. "Hey, that's not a microphone."

We laughed, but Miguel lobbed the joint at her feet and snapped at me, "What the fuck are you laughing at, *güero*?"

"Zuriaa's joke," I said. I looked at Antonio for help, but he turned away.

Miguel leaned in closer, raking me with his bloodshot eyes. "Her *joke*, huh?"

"*Sí*, I laughed at her joke." I tried to stay calm and keep eye contact, as one might stare down a cougar.

After several awkward seconds, Miguel grinned.

"You forgot what I said?" Zuriaa asked.

He smirked, but finally slackened and reached for a *caguama*.

"Shit, that's some good weed, Antonio… You know, maybe I'll hitch to Peru from here—oh, damn. I can't. Not with my briefcase." He looked at me. "*Güero*, you've seen nothing in your life until you've seen Machu Picchu."

"I went there six years ago," I said.

Miguel grabbed Antonio's arm. "Of course, he did!" he shouted. "These fucking *gringos* explore the world, don't they, Antonio?"

Antonio disregarded him and fiddled with his guitar.

Miguel continued, "They bomb and steal from Third World countries and then we host them when they visit our ruins!"

I tried to speak calmly as I peeled the label off the empty *caguama*, but I was thinking of whipping the bottle into his face. "Trust me, I'm broke. I can't even afford to go home."

"Without money, a *gringo* cannot be in Mexico, not legally. So, why are you with us then, huh?"

"Oh, leave him alone!" Zuriaa shouted.

"No. I want to see his passport. Now! Why are you here? Are you a spy? Or did you run away? What did you run from, *güero*? I'll bet it's your family."

"Go fuck yourself!" I shouted, then lobbed the empty bottle in his lap. It rolled to the floor and made a pathetic clanking noise.

"*¡Ya!*" Púas shouted and stood. "Everybody calm down." He opened the door. "David, come with me."

•

Away from the room's sewage stench, Púas and I leaned on the balcony rail and breathed in the cool, sobering air.

"What was that shit about my family?" I asked.

"Don't worry about that *pendejo*. If he gets in your face again, I'll take care of it." Púas put up his fists. "I'm a boxer."

"A boxer?" He looked like one, really—like a boxer from a black-and-white 1940s photograph.

"*Sí*," he said, his shadowboxing waking the dog. "I trained with the Mexican Olympic team two years ago."

"Let's let this dog loose," I said. "Walk him to a taco stand and feed him *chorizo* and *carne asada*."

He laughed. "*¿Neta?* Is that a joke?"

It didn't matter. The dog looked up at me with feral eyes, as if to say, if you reach for my chain, I'll bite off your fingers.

"*Güero*, are you going to Veracruz with Antonio?"

"Yeah."

"We should go north instead. Zuriaa will come, too."

"What about Antonio?"

"Fuck Antonio. The guy's *una lacra*. He didn't have your back in there."

I didn't want to admit it, but Antonio not sticking up for me had really pissed me off. Up until then, I had looked up to him—untethered and unshackled. He was more free than anyone I'd ever known.

"I'm broke," I said. "I don't have any other way to make money."

The door swung open, and Miguel, with his jacket on, came out of the room. "Careful around my dog," he said. "It bites." He turned down the hallway, and we watched him stumble to his room.

•

The next morning, we hid in the shade of a concrete patio at a family restaurant in San Juanito and ate fava bean soup and tortilla chips—the only thing we could afford. Seated across from me, Zuriaa beaded another crappy bracelet. Antonio and Púas sat on either side of us. A white kitten with cruddy eyes rubbed itself against my legs. It purred when I petted it with my feet. I didn't tell the others about the cat. They wouldn't have cared.

"We can leave for Veracruz tomorrow," Antonio said. "My guitar's ready."

"Zuriaa and I will meet you in Veracruz," Púas said. "I need her to come to Mexico City with me today."

"What for?" Antonio asked.

Púas set his coffee down. "I called my aunt yesterday—told her Zuriaa's pregnant."

Antonio nearly dropped his fork. "Are you pregnant?"

"Of course not." Zuriaa wrung her wet hair, letting it drip onto the ground.

"I asked my aunt for five thousand pesos for an abortion," Púas said. "I'm meeting her at the Mexico City bus terminal tonight. It'd be better if Zuriaa came along. My aunt's a lawyer—she trusts nobody, not even me."

I suspected Púas was only trying to lure Zuriaa away from Antonio and their plans for Veracruz, but Antonio looked intrigued. He made a slicing gesture with his right hand across his left palm. "You gonna chip in with these five thousand pesos?"

"Of course," Púas said.

But I knew he was lying, and after we dropped Púas and Zuriaa off at the station, I was certain I'd never see them again.

CHAPTER TEN

Antonio's guitar wasn't ready until the evening. We smoked the rest of our weed and hung around the *zócalo* all day. After we got his guitar back, I didn't ask how much the repairs and lustrous, black paint job had cost him, but it did seem odd to me—to spend money on something like that. We didn't have dinner that night.

Later, we entered an old *cantina*—a dark hole-in-the-wall with saloon-style doors, and got drunk on *caguamas* and shouted over the music.

"We'll leave for Veracruz in the morning!" he said. "Púas will come back with five thousand pesos. Five thousand pesos!"

"You really think they're coming back?" I asked.

"Of course! I was wrong about him. But he's like Pancho Villa. He'll share with us—because, you see, I sense a fusion happening in Veracruz, between *bandas* from all over Mexico! We'll meet Faustina there. She owes me some mushrooms. She and I were drawn to one another on the Pacific, you see. That tension between us is why my wife left. Listen, write this in your book: One night I ate shrooms with Faustina and we swam in the ocean... After a while, we stared in opposite directions—she spaced out on the sky, and I zoned out on the ocean. The waves stopped. I saw a black hole out there, sucking the water down like a drain. And Faustina said she could see a hole in the sky, drawing up the clouds... They were portals! She even heard voices in the sky!" Antonio nodded to himself. His mind was made up. "Yes, we make six thousand pesos in Veracruz, then we eat peyote in the desert. First the material basis, then the spiritual superstructure!"

Antonio watched me check to make sure my recorder was still going, and flashed a big smile. "You gonna write about me?"

"Maybe."

Then I heard a white man speaking broken Spanish to the bartender. He had come in and sat alone at the bar—a bony guy in his fifties who smoked cigarettes and laughed a lot.

"He must spend the winters down here," I said.

Antonio agreed. "He must be rich. Tell you what, I'm going to step out to buy some weed. Why don't you hang around him—see if you can squeeze a few *dolares* out of the guy?"

Antonio looked at me seriously, as though bilking money out of strangers was part of my job description. "How am I supposed to do that?" I asked.

"You're the writer," he said. "Make up a story. Tell him you're broke. *Chale*, tell him the truth! Or, tell him you got robbed."

Antonio gave me twenty pesos to get me started. He said he'd be gone for an hour.

I sat at the bar next to the white man with a patchy beard and a greasy, black ponytail. I ordered a beer, and we got to talking. His name was Eddie. He was a friendly American guy and just looked happy to have someone to talk to.

When my beer was nearly done, the bartender asked if I wanted another. I said I was out of money, and when Eddie learned about how broke I was and how far I'd come and how far I needed to go, he ordered each of us a beer and a shot of tequila. I told him about Mac, getting punched in the eye, hitchhiking, Bella Chevalier, and how I wanted to polish *Curriculum Vitae* on the farm. And then Eddie ordered us more tequila, and we really started talking.

Eddie liked that I was a writer. He let me record our conversation and said I could write a book about him one day. I forgot about bumming money from him, which I wasn't sure I'd find the nerve to do anyway, and instead worried about squeezing stories out of him.

"How long have you been down here?" I asked.

"About five years. Been here since a client of mine overdosed at my Hermosa Beach pool party."

"A client?"

"I was dealing smack," he said. "Judge threw me out of California."

I moved my recorder closer to him. "Threw you out? How does that work?"

Now he looked deflated, like someone had sucked the air out of him. "Don't ask *me*."

"Alright," I said. "Can you tell me a *funny* story instead?"

Eddie lit a cigarette, held two fingers up to the bartender and said, "*Dos más*." Then he pulled the recorder even closer to himself. "Alright, this one time, in the '70s, my girlfriend and I drove to Six Flags. We happened to find two hits of acid in her freezer that weekend. They'd sat in there for a year, so we thought they'd be duds, but we took 'em anyway. And man, did I ever wish we'd split a hit."

We held our new shot glasses. It was our fifth shot, and my mouth flooded with saliva at its smell. I took a deep breath and downed it.

Eddie continued. "Now, the strangest part of the story is this group of retar—now, I guess you can't call them retards... They were... Downs! Downspeople! Roughly ten of them there, these Downspeople, and their caretakers."

I laughed. "*Downspeople?*"

"Anyway, we went up this ride called the Cliffhanger or some shit. It took us straight up, two hundred feet. And we were all on there, my girlfriend, me, and the Downspeople."

"Wait," I said. "They wouldn't take them on that ride."

"We are talkin' late '70s here."

I looked at Eddie through watery eyes. "I didn't eat much today. I think I'm gonna puke."

"Huh? Eat some macadamia nuts! Anyway, the damned thing dropped us, and I screamed all the way down." Eddie's eyes widened, holding the imaginary safety bar in front of him—his hands trembling. "And I do mean, *all the way down*. You ain't never heard nobody scream this loud before in your life."

I stood and prepared to run to the washroom.

Eddie continued, "When we got to the bottom, I was hyperventilating. My hands were white from squeezing. And then, a Six Flags worker ran after the caretakers to tell them someone got left behind. They took me for a Downsperson!"

"That's not what they're called!" I ran to the washroom, ready to puke, but it was locked.

"Well, you know...an individual from the Downs community," he yelled after me. "Where ya goin'? I ain't finished my story 'bout the Cliffhanger."

I burst through the saloon door, stumbled outside, bent over the sidewalk, and unleashed my guts. Disgusted groans came from two women across the street, while a clang of laughter came from inside the bar. Afterwards, I stood and took deep breaths in the evening air, waving to the two tourist-looking ladies who had walked away but looked behind. They didn't wave back. With the cooler evening air hitting my sweaty face, I felt relief. And I was eager for Antonio to get back with some weed.

But he didn't come. So, I sat at the bar again with Eddie, and he had a fresh Corona waiting for me.

I sipped it carefully.

Later, a local man they called Pilas Bajas strolled up to the bar. He had dark skin, scraggly salt-and-pepper hair, and a thin moustache. Eddie said Pilas regularly cruised the *zócalo*, wearing the same grey pants and brown dress shirt, shoeless, with a violin slung over his shoulder in a red Coca-Cola sack.

The bartender explained, "Pilas used to play in the Mexican National Symphony Orchestra, 'til one of the strings in his brain snapped. Now he busks for tourists. And he hates tourists."

Pilas ordered two shots of tequila at once. He stared straight ahead and ignored my *"Buenas tardes."* I slouched on my stool. He slapped a few coins on the bar, threw his shots back, then walked over to a German couple seated at a table and serenaded them with *Les Yeux Noirs* on his violin.

I slammed my hand against the bar. "Damn, that guy can play."

"Ah, screw Pilas, man," Eddie shouted as he spun on his stool to face the bar. "I dropped money in his tip jar yesterday and he threw it on the floor. The sonofabitch is completely *loco*... I'd love to shove his violin straight up his ass... What are you laughing for?"

"I'm picturing you trying to shove a violin up his ass."

"I'd sure as hell get the bow up there!" Eddie said, which cracked me and the bartender up. "Motherfucker's cold-shouldered me for two years."

Later, from the washroom, I heard the tone of the German couple's conversation change to one of trepidation. The violin stopped. Then came a terrible crash. For some reason, I thought Eddie had had a heart attack and fallen off his stool.

I opened the door to find Pilas and Eddie writhing on the floor like salted leeches. I peeled Eddie off Pilas, who lay on his back, while his violin cowered under a table. I put my hand out to help him up, but he hissed like a cat, swatted my hand, and scratched me with his grimy fingernail. He picked himself up, stormed off with his violin tucked under his arm, and cursed at someone on the street.

The bartender handed Eddie some ice for his nose, which was red and dripping blood.

"What happened?" I asked.

"The old bastard screamed in my face, '*¡Odio a los Gringos!*' I know what that shit means. I told him to fuck off, and then he punched me in the mouth. I got some good ones in there, though!" Then he pulled dentures out of his mouth and inspected them with trembling fingers.

"Dentures!" the bartender said. "All dis time, I thinking you has perfect teeth!"

Eddie bought us one last round. And in the silence of the empty bar—everyone gone but us, Eddie's nose no longer bleeding, I wondered if Antonio would ever come back, or if he'd gone back to San Juanito to steal my backpack and I'd be left alone on the Oaxaca streets with ten pesos and no passport or wallet. I turned to Eddie, resolved to ask him for help, when he pulled out his torn-up wallet. There were several bills in there—green two-hundred-peso bills and at least two or three brown five-hundred-peso notes.

"I gotta show you somethin'," he said, sliding out an old photograph and closing his wallet. He handed me the photo.

"Holy fuck!" I said. "Is that you?"

He laughed. "Yes, sir."

He had short hair and was much bigger. "How heavy were you?"

"I was two-fifty with a meth addiction."

Then he opened up his wallet again and handed over a worn-out, folded-up paper torn from a notepad. The writing looked written with his toes.

"That's my suicide note," he said.

"I can't read the writing." I handed it back like it was a brittle artifact.

"I like to keep it around, just to read it once in a while... Mostly 'cause it's funny. Listen: *I ain't got no good reason not to live no more.*" He laughed. "I wrote that, with a loaded Ruger Blackhawk .38 Special on the table. And you know what? I got hung up on the goddamn grammar." He cracked up again—deep laughter, sprung from somewhere in his sadness.

And I was back to being too shy about asking him for money.

"Eddie, you *have* a good reason to live," I said, even though I didn't know.

"Well, I appreciate that, but..."

"Maybe your reason to live is... You're a character in a book I'll write one day."

Eddie flashed a big smile. "You wanna immortalize me?"

"Yes. Yes, I do."

"You know why you write, don't you?"

I shook my head.

"To immortalize *yourself*—leave a piece of you behind, like carving your name in a tree, so you can feel better 'bout dyin' one day and maybe you don't go crazy like the rest of us."

"Eddie, are you going crazy?"

"Goin', goin', gone," he said. Then he leaned into my recorder and whispered, "Make me live forever, too. Wait. No. Shit. No. I... I don't know."

When the bartender stopped serving, Eddie said it was time for him to shut her down, too. I shook his hand and thanked him for the drinks, and then he walked out of the bar, and I had never felt so alone.

The bartender needed to close. So, with Antonio gone for over two hours, and realizing I'd have to walk back to San Juanito on my own, I dragged myself out of the bar. That's when I saw Antonio coming up the street.

•

He said he got tied up waiting for some dealer's connection to come through. But he'd scored a small *tubo*, and we smoked a joint on the way back to our room, and I told him about my night as we stumbled through the crooked side streets, crossing the empty market lot where dogs feasted from a pile of plastic garbage bags—a gloomy setting in the middle of the night, somewhere you'd expect to get stabbed, so I was happy to not be walking alone. Antonio asked if I'd pried any money off Eddie, and I said the guy could only afford to get me drunk, and that I'd barfed on the sidewalk. He laughed, then he shouted and rambled on about his night and his life in general, and I held up my tape recorder, chasing after him like a tenacious reporter. "Do you realize, my wife has sucked the life out of me for months? You see? She dug her hooks into me, to drag herself along. But I need my strength! I need to tear my wife's anchor from me. I need a shaman. I need a voodoo doll to stab in the eyes. I have to save myself, or we're fucked!"

"What are you talking about?"

"Bad vibes. Bad timing, you see? Life's all about timing. How else could you have met me? You could have ended up in Acapulco. But I have to lead you to Veracruz and up to Mazatlán, after Real de Catorce." He shouted into my recorder. "David! Can you hear me, far away, writing a book? You'll never forget me, David! Ahhhh! You'll never forget my raspy voice!"

CHAPTER ELEVEN

In the morning, Antonio and I hitched a ride with a trucker who dropped us off outside Veracruz, in a neighbourhood called El Tejar. From there, we walked for a couple of hours and smoked the rest of our weed. By the time we entered the city, we were too worn out to busk. So in Plaza de Armas, Antonio and I found shade by a cluster of palm trees. Antonio slept on the ground, his sunglasses on and his guitar across his chest, while I sprawled out on a concrete planter.

I dreamed I walked in the shadows of a pine forest, approaching the shores of a great body of water where a group of strangers stood talking and laughing with my father. When I approached him, everyone walked away. He followed them, walking past me. I said, "Dad." He looked over, but kept walking as he said, "Oh, hi. I haven't seen *you* in a while." Then a flood of muddy water rushed toward me, alone now in the forest. The water swept up the leaves and moss, snapped branches, and uprooted trees, which slammed against one another, beating like war drums.

I woke to four black men playing congas nearby. Three large black women, clad in green-and-yellow dresses, bounced their huge hips and sang with powerful church-bell voices that rang across the *zócalo*. A large crowd encircled them, rounding into the long shadows of the cathedral.

"It's called *punta*. They're Hondurans." Antonio spoke with his eyes closed, and wouldn't sit up for the performance.

After every song, the crowd dumped change into a young Mexican woman's sack. It looked heavy. She was shoeless and had short black hair that looked like she'd cut it herself. She wore frayed jean shorts and a black, sun-bleached Zapatista T-shirt snug on her lean body. She danced with the Hondurans with unfettered zeal, her eyes closed, and an enormous smile on her pretty face. There was a wonderful sense of rootlessness about her.

"I think I'm in love with this woman," I said.

Antonio sat up and looked. He yanked off his sunglasses. "It's her... *¡Oye!* Faustina!"

Faustina handed her sack to one of the Honduran women, stopped dancing, and pranced through the crowd, skipping toward us on her tiptoes. Antonio stood and made a move to hug her, but she backed off and wiped the sweat from her chest.

"Sorry, I'm too hot. How have you been?" she asked in a voice that was nasal, but somehow sexy.

"*Bien, bien.* I knew we'd see you here... We went to Oaxaca. Oh, this is David. He's from Canada."

"Hi, nice to meet you," I said, in Spanish.

"Where'd you learn Spanish?" she asked, as her weight shifted in my direction.

"Travelling. I'm French Canadian. The languages are similar."

"I'd like to speak French," she said.

"Look, I bought bongos," Antonio said, holding up the bongos and interrupting the gaze Faustina and I had been sharing. "We're going to Real de Catorce. Where are you going from here?"

As Antonio rambled, I watched Faustina's eyes stray back to the Hondurans.

"Listen, good to see you," she said. "But I have to dance. I'm working with them. Nice to meet you, David."

She hopped away.

Who could blame her? She had found a better *banda*. The Hondurans were pulling in real money, putting on a real show. I thought of asking her if I could join the Hondurans—have them teach me *punta*.

"Hey," Antonio shouted. "You still owe me some mushrooms!"

Faustina stopped. She spun back around, dug into a teeny pocket in her shorts, and lobbed something to Antonio, who missed the catch. As Faustina skipped back to the drummers, Antonio picked the ball of newspaper off the ground and unraveled it slowly. A smirk appeared on his face, as if he'd unwrapped a love letter. He handed me two fat stems and a mushroom cap.

•

In twenty minutes, the shrooms hit my empty stomach. The lights, heat, wind, the clamour of children, dogs, trumpets, and whistles—all came in glittering waves—all the things surging and colliding, then waning in a collective deep breath, before another vibrant exhalation that made me feel happiness and sickening apprehension all at once.

Near sunset, as the crowd left the *zócalo*, Faustina hung around chatting with the Hondurans. One of them was teaching her how to spin fire poi, whirling a fuel-soaked wick around to produce mesmeric swirls in the evening light.

"Looks like they make a lot of money," I said.

Antonio scoffed. "She's degrading herself with this circus act!"

I lay my head on the concrete, hiding behind my sunglasses, and observed my brain somehow processing Antonio's language better than I ever had. I turned on my recorder while he babbled on.

"Look how she flirts with those guys," he said. "She thinks she's queen of the bees!"

I began to think that Antonio had only come all this way for Faustina. He'd probably left his wife for her. He settled for Zuriaa, then Zuriaa dumped him for Púas, and now he had nothing.

"She must have fallen into a portal," he said. "Remember my story about the holes in the ocean and the sky? The portals? They can trap you."

I thought of Mac and how different he'd seemed. How lost. How trapped. Somewhere along the way, had something inside of him shattered? Had he gone too far and been swallowed into a void?

The mushroom trip had begun its descent when Zuriaa and Púas appeared, smiling and brimming with joy. He wore a new duckbill hat and ran around snapping photos of women with a disposable camera. She carried a bag of *tamales* and apple sodas to share with us. Antonio and I didn't eat, and we didn't mention Faustina or the mushrooms.

"How did Mexico City go?" Antonio asked.

"I saw my mom!" Zuriaa said.

"Your *mother*?"

"Yeah, he took me to see her."

"What are you saying? What about his rich aunt?" Antonio asked.

"Why so many questions? Check out these beads and stuff Púas bought me!" She showed us the steel wire, cat's-eye beads, and dried coconut shells.

"Look at that *pendeja*!" Antonio stood in a huff and snatched his backpack off the ground.

"What?" Zuriaa looked up, thinking Antonio was talking to her—but he had noticed Faustina walk away with the Hondurans.

He seemed to have already forgotten about Zuriaa and Púas. "Fuck it, David. You know what? My old friends always ask me how I stay slim, why I look this young... And I tell them it's because I keep moving. I keep rolling, you see? We'll hang around here a few days, then head to Villarmosa. I have an aunt there. After that, I think we should go down to Guatemala."

"*South?*" I asked. "What about Real de Catorce?"

He swung his backpack onto his back. "Non-attachment, David. See, I have a new mantra: *Om ah hung vajra guru pema siddhi hung*... Say it ten million times and you'll turn into fucking light! Hurry, *banda*, let's set up camp on the beach. Can you hear the crowd? I think the parade's starting." He grabbed his guitar and walked away.

•

The crowd had gathered by the Gulf of Mexico at the Gran Plaza del Malecón. There were cargo ships, souvenir stands, mariachis, balloons, and swooping seagulls shitting all over the place. Along Boulevard Manuel Ávila Camacho, two rows of bleachers stretched out farther than we could see. Ahead of the coming parade, hundreds of people swarmed toward us like zombies, in search of empty seats.

Antonio pointed to the mob. "We'll have to walk through them to reach the beach." He moved forward, alone, like a man about to walk off a bridge. The horde swallowed him. Púas leaped into the frenzy. Zuriaa followed.

I looked back to the *zócalo* and its relative calmness—children chasing pigeons, and smiling lovers lounging at sidewalk cafes—where I wanted to ride out the rest of my mushroom trip. I wanted to tear myself away from Antonio's vortex before it dragged me further and further away from Ignacio's farm.

Zuriaa shouted, "Are you coming, *güero*? I already lost the guys."

When I saw her youthful face in the mob, like a lighthouse in the fog, I hugged the bongos and moved toward her.

•

Everyone shouted and sweated and stepped over one another—children clung to their parents through the stench of booze and gunpowder. I struggled to keep up with Zuriaa, who called for Antonio and Púas. Then I quickly lost sight of her. Fireworks went off and fizzled in the distance. Some idiot threw a firecracker at my feet and it went off like a bomb. I froze, dripping sweat and stumbling in a state of confusion. I felt everyone come at me from every corner. I felt my backpack pulled sideways, and caught a guy with his hand on my bag. I gave him a dirty look, and he vanished. Finally, I spotted Antonio and Zuriaa. They seemed to be arguing; their arms flailed in the menacing dusk.

"Púas!" I shouted when I saw him in the crowd.

We walked together.

"Your tent's falling off," he shouted over the noise, as he reached under my backpack and pulled my tent out with ease. "Some *pendejo* cut one of your straps!"

"*¡Hijo!* I saw the fucker," I said, looking back.

He tucked my tent under his arm. "Let's not start anything here."

"I'm all fucked up," I said. "Don't leave me."

He didn't hear me. "Let's dump these *mamones*, *güero*."

"What?"

"I've got money," he shouted. "We'll take a bus to Mazatlán. I'll work on the farm with you while you finish your book. I'll have my work visa in a couple of months, I can come with you whenever you drive back to Canada."

"Púas!" Zuriaa shouted from a distance.

Púas followed her deeper into the crowd, still carrying my tent. I lost them, but I walked with renewed purpose. Traveling with Púas, there would be no more distractions.

"David!" Zuriaa shouted. She stood on the bleachers, waving me over from within the horde.

"Where's Púas?" I asked.

"Antonio took him to buy some weed," she said.

We squeezed through a narrow passage between the stands and onto the boardwalk.

"*¡Chingao!*" she shouted. Two paramedics were attending to a man who had fallen from the top bleacher. He lay unconscious in front of us, breathing rapidly, his hair soaked in a small pool of blood. His Mexican-flag baseball cap had settled upright on the boardwalk.

We had to step over his legs, and I said, "That's a lot of blood."

Zuriaa let out a big laugh. "That's his beer, *idiota!*" She jumped from the boardwalk onto the beach.

With each step through the cooling sand, the noise and the mushrooms faded. We dumped our bags and sat by the water, kicked our shoes off, and watched the Gulf's tiny waves twirl in.

In the distance, the crowd cheered.

Zuriaa tilted her head back to look upside-down at the boardwalk and bleachers. "The parade's coming." She turned to me and asked, "Were you afraid back there, *güero*? You looked afraid."

"I hate crowds. Someone tried to cut my tent off my backpack."

"What? *Crowds*? How will you be a writer if you're afraid of crowds?" She cracked up, unable to contain her amusement.

"Did Púas take you to see his aunt?" I asked.

Her face turned red, and she looked to the sky with a huff. "He doesn't have an aunt in Mexico City," she said. "The fucker took me to see my mom in Toluca."

"Why?"

"Last week, she gave him three thousand pesos to track me down. Anyway, she gave me two thousand pesos 'cause I promised her I'd come back home and go to school."

"So, why'd you come back?"

"'Cause I'm not going to school! I just want to keep travelling!" she said. "I want to go to Real de Catorce, man. I want to see the desert, and then I want to see the jungles and pyramids in Chiapas. Anyway, my mom gave Púas money, too. Just to keep an eye on me.

He's just like Antonio. They think they're my fucking bodyguards." She rolled over in the sand, looked into my eyes, and said, "Your eyes are blue, blue, blue!"

I knew what she was thinking, so I said, "Does it feel strange you dated Púas, then Antonio, and now Púas again, and they're both here?"

She howled, rolled back over, and pounded the sand. "Oh, *güero*, you're so *ingenuo*."

I'd never heard that word.

She turned to face me again. "How tall are you, *güero*, a hundred and eighty?"

"I don't know—not in centimetres," I said.

"I've always had tall boyfriends. I wonder why."

"Maybe you're still growing."

•

I recognized Faustina's short haircut right away. She sat on a log by the fire with a couple with dreadlocks and congas at their feet. They invited us to join them. When Faustina asked about Antonio, Zuriaa coolly said we'd lost him, and then she went off to pitch her tent, which took her a while. I sat beside Faustina, slipped off my shoes, and dug my feet into the soft sand. She had little feet, with pretty, brown toes. Her friendly eyes made her easy to talk to, but when she wasn't smiling, she looked terribly preoccupied.

Soon, music battered our eardrums as the parade rolled by fifty feet away. I shared our cold *tamales* with Faustina and her friends, and they got me stoned. As the evening went on, I kind of forgot about Antonio. Faustina and I sat close, closer than we needed to, but somehow, it made sense, like our coupling had been established without the necessary chase.

When they ran out of beer, Faustina and I left to find more.

On the boardwalk, she ran to a vendor and bought a novelty-sized plastic mug filled with draft beer. She took a sip and handed it to me. "Here. You need to catch up!" I drank while she scanned the seats for a way to get through.

"The liquor store is on the other side." She pointed to the buildings across the street. "*¡Oye!*" She called up to two men standing on plastic chairs set up on the boardwalk. The men looked down to her, and without hesitation, pulled her up over the backs of their chairs. She climbed the next row and vanished.

The men reached down, and I clasped the giant beer mug with both hands as they pulled me up by my elbows and armpits. Everything dazzled: the colourful floats, camera flashes, costumes, music, marimbas, drums... It felt incredible to be a part of whatever they were celebrating.

Several rows ahead, Faustina climbed over chairs, tapping shoulders, and everyone made way for her. "I'm with her," I shouted. Everyone cleared a path for me to climb over their chairs with my enormous beer in hand.

When I reached the last row, Faustina darted alongside the floats. I tried to hurry, but slipped on a chair and spilled half my beer down a woman's back.

I shouted, "*¡Lo siento!*" But she only cared about dancing with her friends.

I tossed the mug to the street and ran to where Faustina danced near the floats.

The parade slowed, and Faustina bolted for a space between two floats. "Run!" she shouted. I ran after her, but feather-clad dancers blocked us from pushing our way through. The floats rolled again. Caught between the floats, we moved along with the performers, surrounded by their choreography. "Blend in!" she shouted. "Dance!" She danced, and I hopped around and pretended to dance until I finally was dancing. I felt like I had met Antonio and Zuriaa on the coast only so they could lead me to this moment with Faustina. I thought of kissing her, but two policemen on the sidewalk were pointing at us.

I forced my way through the dancers, and Faustina followed.

Across the street, we crawled under the bleachers to the sidewalk, then walked a couple of blocks along rows of palm trees, until we found a liquor store. Faustina bought a bottle of tequila.

We crossed the street after the parade passed. A group of women on the bleachers called out, "*¡Güero!*"

I walked away, but Faustina stopped. "Hey, go talk to them!" She pointed at one of the women. "Look at this one. She's pretty."

I approached the tall Mexican woman and introduced myself. A group of men behind her observed our small talk, and they chanted for us to kiss, "*¡Beso! ¡Beso!*" I turned to Faustina, and she joined in the chant, "*¡Beso! ¡Beso! ¡Beso!*" I leaned in and kissed the tall woman on the cheek. Then the guys at the back chanted, "*¡Puto! ¡Puto! ¡Puto!*" Before the entire bleacher section joined in, I leaned in and kissed the woman on the mouth. Everyone cheered, including Faustina, who then spoke into my ear, "I was starting to think you were gay."

•

We sat at the fire for a while, drinking tequila out of plastic cups. Zuriaa had come out of her tent to scan the boulevard and beach for Púas and Antonio. It was late—the chaos of the parade having dissipated into the night—and I spotted Antonio's dark figure, walking alone down the beach. He lugged his backpack and dragged his guitar across the sand like a child pulling a toy through a sandbox.

Zuriaa and I went to Antonio.

He was sobbing. "It's shit! It's all shit!"

"Where's Púas?" I asked.

"They stabbed him."

Zuriaa and I stopped walking. Antonio wiped his tears away and kept moving.

I felt my guts want to empty themselves. "Where is he?"

"Who knows? I got lost."

"Where were you?" Zuriaa asked.

"We got lost!" He arrived at the fire, dropped his bag, stole my seat beside Faustina, and introduced himself to her friends.

Zuriaa went to him—her hands planted heavily on her hips. "Antonio, where's Púas?"

Everyone waited silently for an answer.

"We followed a Colombian guy. He led us into an alleyway somewhere. Six guys jumped us. One of them had a knife. He stabbed Púas. The last thing I remember is him screaming, 'Run! Run!' He has all that cash on him, too. They probably took it. That's why I wanted him to come with me, you see. I knew he had all that money and I wanted to score."

Zuriaa's voice quivered. "You left him." Then she stormed off to her tent.

Antonio didn't flinch. Instead, he lit half a joint, took a couple of hauls, and handed it over to me. Nobody spoke. Nobody knew what to do. Faustina tossed the rest of her drink onto the coals, and they hissed. Then she and her friends said goodnight and went to their tents.

I took a drag and handed the joint back to Antonio. "When did you find weed?"

He smoked and stared into the fire. "At one point, a guy held my guitar in the air, ready to trash it, but the Colombian guy said, 'No, not the guitar. It's his *chamba*... He must be a guitarist."

"They saved your guitar, but they killed Púas?"

No answer. His story wasn't making any sense.

"Did you score from the Colombian *before* he stabbed Púas?" I asked.

Still no answer.

And instead of talking about what had happened, or what might happen next, Antonio moved away to pitch his tent and then crawled inside. I was convinced Púas was still out there, that Antonio had given him the slip.

I stayed up alone, drinking from Faustina's tequila bottle. The clouds slithered in to choke out the stars one by one. I waited for Púas to find me sitting alone by the dwindling fire, and later hoped Faustina would come out of her tent, but she never came out. Then I remembered Púas had my tent—my four-hundred-dollar North Face tent—the only thing in my backpack worth selling. I rested my head on the beach. The ground spun... I dug my hand into the sand and held on.

•

I woke to strong winds and panicked voices. I crawled from out of my bag, with my head pounding.

Sand whipped my face. Antonio stood alone on the beach, stuffing his tent in his backpack.

"What's going on?"

"*¡Un huracán!*" he shouted.

Black clouds, like ashes coughed from a volcano, loomed over the shivering Gulf water. We shielded our faces from the lashing wind and sand.

"*Pinche güero,* you almost slept through a hurricane!" It was Faustina.

We carried our backpacks off the beach as the rain came and we walked through colourful plastic cups, cans, and plates that blew across the boardwalk like dead autumn leaves.

Antonio walked ahead of us. "*Vamonos.* The hurricane's coming."

"Where's Zuriaa?" I asked. Antonio didn't hear me, or didn't want to answer.

"She's gone," Faustina said. "I talked to her this morning before she left."

"Where did she go?"

"She's taking a bus to Chiapas. Then she's going home, back to school. She looked pretty sad. I mean, obviously with what happened to your other friend."

"He wasn't killed," I said. "Antonio's story is ridiculous. Can I join your group for a while? Are you guys going north? Púas is probably on his way home to Toluca with my tent. We need to get to my friend's farm near Mazatlán."

"The Hondurans left for Villahermosa this morning," she said. "I'm going to Real de Catorce—that's kind of on the way."

I smiled, and we agreed to hitchhike north together in the morning.

By the time we entered the *zócalo*, people said the hurricane alert had been downgraded to a tropical storm. Nonetheless, we were soaked and starving all day, smoking joints, huddled in a storefront alcove. My manuscript, tucked at the bottom of my bag, had gotten wet. I removed the pages from my soaking sweater and rolled them up in my dry, dirty T-shirts.

Antonio didn't say anything about Faustina and me, but I didn't care anyway. I'd come all this way for his fusion of *bandas*, and I didn't have a peso to show for it. And now I'd lost my tent.

CHAPTER TWELVE

Faustina and I woke at night, with Antonio leaning over us.

"This is Victor," he said. "He's taking us to his house." Victor wore a black raincoat. He looked about thirty years old. He had a cookie-cutter face—flat and forgettable. A face like a mannequin, with painted brown eyes, a carved grin, and short hair parted to the side.

The storm hadn't stopped, so the thought of sleeping under a roof got us up fast. Antonio and Victor walked ahead of us, and Faustina and I followed them through the pelting raindrops.

"How far do you live?" Antonio asked.

I couldn't understand Victor's mumbling.

A few blocks later, Antonio asked again.

"Five minutes away," he said.

"Victor, you said that fifteen minutes ago," Antonio said.

"My name's not Victor. It's Raphael."

I wanted to stop, to stay away from this lunatic and take our chances anywhere else, but Faustina and Antonio walked on, so I followed.

Fifteen minutes must have passed by the time we came to an intersection, where the street flowed like a muddy creek.

"We have to take a bus from here," Raphael said.

"I thought you lived five minutes away?" I asked.

We backed off a few steps and left Raphael waiting at the bus stop.

Antonio whispered, "He keeps changing his name. I think he has multiple personalities or something."

Faustina shivered. "I don't care what his name is. I'm soaked. I need to sleep inside tonight."

The prospect of sleeping in a house with Faustina filled me with courage. "He's not dangerous," I said. "There are three of us. We'll be fine."

•

An overcrowded bus finally pulled over. Raphael, Faustina, and I squeezed onto the stairs as much as we could, but Antonio only had one foot in the doorway when the bus began to move. He held on to the handle with one hand, guitar in the other, and hopped alongside the bus.

"Wait!" I shouted. But the weight of Antonio's bag pulled him down.

"¡Para!" I shouted.

Faustina shrieked, "He fell under the bus!"

Everyone on the bus lurched to the windows and screamed for the driver to stop. Victor, or Raphael, or whatever his name was, stood expressionless.

The driver slammed his brakes, and we all jumped off. I thought we'd find Antonio's head crushed like a watermelon, his body twitching, his guitar splintered like kindling.

But half a block back, Antonio was limping toward us in the rain.

"Did you get run over?" Faustina asked.

"No, it missed me—not like you'd care."

"Stop feeling sorry for yourself," she said.

He ignored her.

"Your guitar's cracked again," I said.

Antonio held it up to have a look. It had broken in the same spot where his wife had bashed a hole. "You see, David? I told you my ex cursed me."

Raphael approached. "My house is close to here. We can walk, if you still want to go."

Faustina snapped, "Where the fuck do you live, man?"

Raphael pointed to an intersection. "I promise. You see those traffic lights? Seven blocks from there."

As the rain slowed, we navigated around dirty puddles on deserted streets until we finally arrived at a row of townhouses.

Raphael unlocked the door and led us into a darkened hallway and flicked on the lights. The living room contained nothing but two old sofas and a small tube television on an end table.

•

After a cool shower upstairs, I found a can of shaving cream under the sink, so I pulled out the dull, rusty blade from my bag. Halfway through my shave, I heard Antonio talking to Faustina downstairs, so I opened the door a crack.

"Let's get rid of him," he said.

"What? Why?"

"Because he's not a traveller like you and me. He doesn't know what it's like to be drawn to the road, to be homesick, even when you're home."

I stood there, shaving and mumbling to myself about Antonio trying to ditch me, when through the mirror, I spotted Raphael watching me from the hallway. I opened the door. He raised his hand and showed me his pocket-sized Bible.

"This is my God," he said. "He speaks to me."

"I need to finish shaving." I shut the door and locked it.

•

I slumped onto the sofa beside Faustina. Antonio sat tuning his guitar on the sofa facing us.

At the sight of my freshly shaved face, Faustina smiled and grabbed my chin, and said, "Now you look like a *güero*." So I figured she hadn't agreed to Antonio's plan to bail on me.

"You guys have to be quiet," Raphael whispered.

"You live with someone?" Antonio asked.

"I live with my sister. She's at work. She's a police officer."

The three of us exchanged glances, then Raphael looked at me like he just realized I was a white guy, and said, "I had a brother who looked just like you."

Antonio chuckled. "Was your brother white?"

Raphael ignored the question. "He had blue eyes. He died of drugs. He went crazy."

"I'm not going crazy," I said.

Raphael began pacing throughout the house, from the living room to the kitchen and back, with his arms hung motionless to his sides, mumbling to himself.

I found a lanyard hung on the banister—Raphael's work I.D. His name wasn't Raphael or Victor. It was Ismael. He worked in a pharmacy.

When Ismael walked upstairs, I showed Antonio and Faustina the I.D., and whispered, "I think he's gotten into some pills. I knew someone like him."

Antonio chuckled. "Maybe he'll share some."

Faustina didn't look amused. "If he's on medication, he probably needs it."

We continued our diagnosis of Ismael, or whatever his name was, until he called downstairs, "The girl can sleep upstairs tonight, in the spare room."

Faustina shook her head.

"It's okay," I said. "We'll all sleep in the living room."

"I want to leave," Faustina whispered. "This guy scares me."

Antonio lay on the sofa and rolled over, turning his back to us. "We're as safe in here as we are outside. But there's a terrible vibe in this city. It attacked me the moment we arrived. We'll head south tomorrow."

•

I had let Faustina have the second sofa, and rolled my sleeping bag on the floor. For a while, I scribbled in my pad—my hunger and frustration of losing Púas and my tent keeping me up.

"Hey, you're not sleeping?" Faustina whispered. "You want to walk outside? It stopped raining."

I dug into my bag, and pulled a two-hundred-peso bill out of my sock.

•

It was 2 a.m. No one else out—not even the dogs. At an OXXO, I bought us two ham-and-cheese sandwiches, a bag of Takis, and a *caguama* of Pacifico. We sat on the curb outside the house and feasted.

"How long were you travelling with Antonio on the Pacific?" I asked, wanting to learn more about how his wife had come to leave him. "He said you two had a mushroom trip in the ocean, and you saw portals in the sky."

"What? That never happened," she said. "I only remember seeing him around."

We kept talking, and I told her about Bella Chevalier, and my plan to edit *Curriculum Vitae* on Ignacio's farm.

She said, "I write too. I leave notes in places for strangers to find."

"Where? What sort of notes?"

Faustina got up to pee, squatting between two parked cars. "Yesterday, I left a note in the women's washroom in the *zócalo*. I wrote about when I was twelve and got hit by a car. I almost died. I was hospitalized for three months and had a tube draining fluid from my lungs. To exercise, the nurses had me inflate balloons every day. By the time I left the hospital, I'd filled the room with colourful balloons." I wrote her story in my notepad and watched her urine snake through the cobblestone cracks and down to a rain puddle, like the fluid from her drowning lungs.

She took the bottle from me, then my notepad. "Can I see?" She had decided I should leave a note somewhere, and sifted through pages of scrambled thoughts written out of order, some sideways or upside down. "Is this English?" she asked. "Did you write all of this? It looks like a bunch of people wrote in here."

I took back my notepad and tore out the first legible page. "Here. It's a poem."

She pointed across the street, to a small shrine someone had hung outside their house off the sidewalk—a weathered wooden frame with a crusty statue of the Virgin of Guadalupe and three burned-out candles. We crossed the street and I folded the poem, reluctant to leave my only copy. But I trusted Faustina, and thought of it as an offering.

"No. Read it to me first," she said.

I tried to translate. "Through a failed sky, the jaw of order put out the night light. And in the earth deceased, bones search for flesh."

"*¡Hijo!*" She pulled me away. "It's so dark. You can't leave that here!"

I slid the poem back into my notepad. "Write a new story," she said. "Write about when you were a kid, something nice, like my balloon story."

I stepped away from Faustina and the shrine, deeper into the night, and the void of my forgotten youth.

"Where you going?" she asked.

"To exchange this *caguama*. I can't think of any stories."

Faustina caught up to me and asked, "You don't remember your childhood?"

"No."

•

In the morning, I woke alone on the floor. For a second, I thought Antonio and Faustina had left me, but then Antonio poked his head out from the doorway. "We're leaving," he said, closing up his backpack, unaware that the night before, when Faustina and I had come back into the house, we'd rooted through the side pockets of his backpack and found two *tubos* of weed, which I now had in my backpack. We'd talked of slipping out before Antonio woke, but now what?

I shoved my sleeping bag into my backpack as Faustina came downstairs with wet hair, dressed and ready to go. She squeezed past Ismael, who sat quietly at the foot of the stairs, forlorn as he watched us pack up.

When we all had our shoes on and stood at the door, Antonio said, "Okay, Victor—Raphael, we're off."

Ismael stood. "Please stay. I'll die without you guys."

I yanked the door open. The three of us shuffled out into the sunny morning. Ismael followed us, barefoot. A vacuous smile spread across his wooden face. "If you go, I'll die." He reached into his pocket and pulled out a TV remote. He squinted as he aimed the remote at the clouds.

"We have to go," Faustina said. She tugged at my shirt.

Walking up the sidewalk, we looked back to see Ismael still standing there, pointing his remote at a distorted grey sky.

•

We took a bus to the *zócalo*, then retraced our steps to the parade.

"Let's go smoke a joint at the beach," Antonio said.

Faustina and I eyed each other, slowing our pace as we neared the parade street still cluttered with garbage. We'd have to leave before Antonio figured out that we'd ripped him off, but I was carrying his bongos and didn't want to steal those too. I began to wonder if I should slip his weed back into his pocket when we got to the beach, where I hoped we'd run into Púas.

Faustina wandered off to find a place to pee.

"Are you writing about me?" Antonio asked.

"What?"

"In your notepads. Do you write about me?"

"Yeah. I'm immortalizing you."

He smiled. "We'll head to Villahermosa today. I have an aunt there. We can regroup for a week, play the *zócalo*." Then he whispered, "When we get rid of this chick, we'll move on to Chiapas."

"Why would we get rid of her?"

"She's not a real traveller—not like us. After Chiapas, we'll go to Guatemala."

"What happened to Real de Catorce? You know I have to get to Mazatlán."

"Don't worry about Mazatlán. We're going to make so much money, you'll fly there. But I have to swing by Chiapas to visit my son."

"Your *son*?"

"Yes. He's three. We named him Williamsii, after the cactus."

As Antonio babbled about the adventures we'd have and the money we'd make, I thought about his son, fatherless in Chiapas. And his wife, whom he'd abandoned like he'd abandoned Púas. And how he'd tried to abandon me, and now Faustina. All of a sudden, I understood why his wife had smashed his guitar with a rock.

We came to a group of men and women seated at the foot of the bleachers. They'd been up all night and were still singing and playing guitar, stinking of stale cigarette smoke and booze. We drank rum and flat Coke with them and smoked weed from their soapstone pipe.

Faustina and I sat together in the bleachers and watched the spectacle. Antonio dropped his backpack and joined when the guys started playing a song that was at once melancholic and happy—a song I'd never heard.

"What song is that?" I asked Faustina.

"*Ojala*. Silvio Rodriguez. You don't know it?"

I shook my head. "That's the kind of music Antonio should have been playing all along." I thought of asking Faustina if she knew Antonio had a son, but I didn't want to ruin the moment. I hadn't seen him look this happy in weeks. I knew that feeling of leaving was in his bones again, because that same feeling now jolted my bones, too.

I turned to Faustina, *"¿Vamonos?"*

She nodded.

We slinked, unnoticed, down the seats like spiders and up the beach.

I'd left Antonio's bongos on the bleachers.

CHAPTER THIRTEEN

Faustina and I caught a ride out of town in a speeding Suburban that dropped us off somewhere along Highway 140. We smoked a joint and walked for three hours, sweat soaking our shirts and pooling under our backpacks, and we talked about finding a place to camp for the evening—both of us knowing we only had her tent.

We approached an old, rusty farm truck parked on the shoulder. The farmer let us sit in the back with big sacks of beans under a blue tarp. I slumped on the bags beside Faustina, who bathed in the heavenly blue light, and I thought of kissing her, but I was too shy. So I peered through the slatted wood walls at the hillside rolling by like a blurred slideshow as we hurtled toward Mexico City and Toluca.

She looked over at me reading pages of my now-soiled manuscript.

"Do you think you write to avoid things?" she asked.

"I don't think so."

"Tell me about your family," she said.

Finally I put away my notepad. By the way she was looking at me, I could see she really did want to know, so I told her about my father's death and about the stroke that had disabled my mother, and about my sister and my little nephew. She loved to hear me talk about my nephew, how he spoke French and English and how everybody said he looked like me, which was to say, he looked like my father.

"It's unfortunate your nephew never met his grandfather," she said. "They'll probably turn out to be similar people. What was your father like?"

"I don't know. Funny, I guess. Athletic. Creative. I just have to make sure my nephew doesn't grow up to work in the mines, like he did."

"You think you'll have kids one day?"

I shook my head. "I'd rather create than procreate."

Faustina gave me a pitiful smile. "Are those really the only options? Couldn't you do both?"

"I don't think I could do both, not *well*."

She looked away. She knew I wanted the conversation to end.

"You think that Victor guy will hurt himself?" she asked.

"Ismael? Hard to tell with *locos*."

"Don't say that," she said, turning her head to look through the slats on her side of the truck. "Don't say *loco*. He's just sick... My mom once put me in an institution." She stopped talking.

I wondered what scars she was remembering then—tears and white sheets and a hospital bed. Was it pills or cuts or a dangling noose? The way she just kept looking outside, I thought she'd rather be out there walking the road alone now, than stuck in here with me—someone who never knew what to say when people needed something to be said.

"Maybe we should budget for this trip," I said. "I've got about four hundred pesos left."

She turned her head slowly, her whole body shrinking with a crestfallen exhale. "Oh, I was hoping you had more. I've only got ninety."

"It looked like you were raking it in with those Hondurans," I said.

"No. They kept the cash."

It got quiet and it stayed quiet for the rest of the ride—both of us realizing we were screwed, with no instruments or any way to make money.

•

Outside Córdoba, it was near dark. We hiked up a steep hill into a village where we asked the locals about places to camp. Someone suggested we ask the Pentecostal church for refuge.

The church was on the main floor of a two-storey duplex on a residential dirt road. A street vendor sold us *elotes*—corn-on-the-cob smeared with mayo and covered in crumbled *cotija* cheese, chili powder, and fresh lime juice. It was the only thing we'd eaten all day, except for a bunch of bananas, and we devoured it on the church's lawn, waiting for the evening service to end.

There were no curtains in the picture window, which allowed us to see inside the narrow, white room: twenty people sat on white plastic folding chairs, listening to the preacher.

"You believe in God?" Faustina asked.

"My grandmother used to say if I didn't believe, baby Jesus would come down from Heaven and eat my toes," I said. "So, I don't know. I'm open to it. But, if there is a god, I wish it wasn't a secret."

The churchgoers began making their way out, shaking hands with a man in black who had oily, black hair and pitted acne scars all over his face. Once everyone had gathered their children and headed toward their cars, we approached him.

Faustina unleashed her smile. She had perfect teeth. "Excuse me, *señor*. We're passing through town, and wondering if you could help us find a place to spend the night."

He looked us over. "*Un momento.*" He went inside and returned a minute later with a white-haired man, someone I assumed was a pastor. He took a good look at us, simply nodded to the man in black, then walked away.

"Everything's fine," the man in black said. "Come inside."

We followed him into the dusty church, and he closed the door. "Please, have a seat." We sat in the chairs, and he sat facing us on the piano bench. The piano behind him looked tortured, with peeled veneer and grubby white keys. He brought his hands together. "We can help. God's will brought you here."

I offered no reaction, but Faustina said politely, "*Gracias, señor.*"

He went on, "The Bible says we are never meant to feel at home because we are not home at all. God instilled that feeling in us, so we want to look for that further something... Do you deny it?" In our uncomfortable silence, he waited for an answer. "There's an empty room upstairs where you can stay, but... are you boyfriend and girlfriend?"

"Why?" I asked.

"Because I can see you're in love, but this is a house of God." He leaned in. "And since you are guests in His house, it's important you abstain from... certain activities." He looked straight at me. "You understand very little Spanish, correct?"

"No. I understand."

He stood abruptly and walked to the front door. "You two look exhausted. I'll leave you to rest." Before he left, he added, "Please leave this door unlocked."

We watched him walk down the street, until his darkness melded with the night.

"Did you get a pedophile vibe off him?" I asked.

Faustina burst out laughing. "*What*? You're ridiculous!"

I locked the deadbolt, then sat at the piano, gently pressing a key, only hard enough to hear a faint note.

"Do you play?" Faustina asked.

"Not really. We used to have an upright like this when I was a kid. My dad used to play. I remember dancing with my sister."

"That's nice," she said. "You see, you do remember your childhood."

My smile went away as quickly as it had appeared.

•

Upstairs, we found the room cluttered with boxes and garbage bags. We pushed things aside and rolled out our sleeping bags, sending dust bunnies sailing across the filthy tiles. Then I turned the light off and we lay in our bags, eighteen inches from each other, surrounded by boxes. We stared at the ceiling in awkward silence.

"You think God would disapprove of us getting high in here?" Faustina asked.

"There's only one way to find out," I said.

She fetched a fat roach from her bag and lit it.

We tried to exhale out the window. "What if there is a God, but no afterlife?" I asked. "You ever think about that? That maybe God gave us this whole life, and yet, most of us still want something more?"

Faustina looked up at me and didn't take her eyes away. "I guess you'd better make the most of this life, David."

It was an invitation—to kiss her, to love her, to roll around on the dirty floor with her. But the joint was only half done, and I wanted to smoke all of it first.

"I was thinking," she said. "Instead of the farm, maybe you could come stay at my place. My parents have a guest house. You'd have the days to yourself, to write. I'll be busy with school."

"What are you studying?"

"Everything. I have to finish high school."

"*High school*? Wait—how old are you?"

It must have been the look on my face that caused her to blush. "Eighteen. Why? How old are you?"

"Twenty-five," I said.

She threw her head back and laughed. "I thought you were, like, my age. How old did you think *I* was?"

"I'd have guessed... *my* age."

She chuckled. "Maybe my year in the institution aged me."

"A *year*?"

A loud thud came from downstairs and stirred my bowels.

"What was that?" she whispered. "You locked the door, right?"

"Yeah."

Another thud. The doorknob rattled downstairs.

Faustina's eyes opened wide. "Someone's trying to get in."

I slipped my shoes on. "It's nothing. Could be next door."

"Where you going?"

"Nowhere. But I want to be ready."

We sat waiting for someone to break in, our hearts pounding in the stillness. But nothing happened.

Faustina eventually fell asleep, but I lay awake for hours with my shoes on. Eighteen years old. And just like that, the excitement I'd felt for Faustina had gone, and all I wanted was to put her on a bus home and to find Púas and be off to Ignacio's farm.

•

We snuck out of the village at daybreak and walked down a highway. There was no shoulder, so we hugged the rock face and trampled over dried weeds, careful not to get clipped by traffic. When we found a shoulder where cars could pull over, we dumped our bags on the slope and got stoned. We had a quarter ounce of weed left, which seemed to be the only thing now keeping us together.

A couple of rides took us into Puebla. We got there late, so we searched for a place to camp and came across a house for sale in an empty, fenced-in lot with overgrown weeds. We climbed over the eight-foot fence. Behind the house, we found a concrete patch with just enough space to pitch Faustina's tent. We tossed our bags inside and headed to the *zócalo*, where Faustina bought a brown bottle of cough syrup.

"Ever get high on this?" she asked.

•

We sat on our bags and smoked a joint, sheltered from the rain that pattered the tent walls. We took turns sipping the purple cough syrup until we drank half the bottle, and then I finished the rest and we settled in for some sort of ride.

Soon, my thoughts became anesthetized, my body lying in a peaceful warmth I thought would carry me into sleep. But a crackle of thunder cued a heavy downpour and the smell of rain filled the tent. As I started to zip the flaps closed, we saw the deluge flooding the yard already. "This will get worse," Faustina said.

She put her shoes on and made a frantic run for the house, the rain soaking her before she found an open window and crawled inside. I gathered our things and ran to the house. Faustina opened the front door. "Welcome home!"

For some reason, the empty two-bedroom house had a hammock strung over the living room floor.

Faustina lay on the tiles and looked comfortable on our dirty sleeping bags and pillows made from our sweaters. She closed her eyes. I took the hammock. Over and over again, came a slipping sensation—a slipping out of consciousness.

Slipping.

Slipping.

Slipping.

Words stumbled out of me, "I feel something. You want the hammock?"

Faustina snored and slobbered on my sweater. I wondered if she'd had a stroke. I thought of my mother, remembered who she was before the stroke permanently rewired her brain—turned her into the woman who struggled to walk, and spent most of her time watching tennis and soap operas. I remembered when I was a boy and she took a part-time job as a recess monitor at my school. From across the schoolyard, I would spy on her, perplexed as to why a flock of girls always followed her around the yard, like they were her ducklings.

The cough syrup high made it nearly impossible to shake the thoughts of my mother out of my head. I felt guilty for being so far from her. I thought, think of this trip as an education. Research. You're a working writer. That's right, you're a businessman. You're not on vacation here; this isn't Captain Hook's Dinner Show.

Then my heart pounded. My body vibrated. And my legs began trembling.

"What the hell, man—relax," I whispered. "It's okay, it's okay. It's not a stroke, you'll be okay... Stop talking to yourself. She'll hear you... I know!" I was hearing myself speak, with no control over my words.

I snuck outside and leaned against the house, sheltered from the heavy rain. Suddenly, I was not there. I knew where I was, and who I was, but I was inside my head, watching this happen to someone else. I whispered, "Come back... You're alright. Come back." I swung my arms around, rubbed my head, and smacked my legs, trying to warm up, to feel connected to my body again, but nothing worked. I stretched my arms to the sky, and a knife slashed at me, slicing my chest. I jumped back, grabbing myself. "What was that?" Nothing had happened. Yet the blade came at me again, cutting me open. "Stop thinking of that. Stop thinking of that!" An image flashed through my head: a rotten mouth with missing and decrepit teeth. "You sonofabitch. No more drugs. No more!" I hopped up and down, determined to continue doing so until I fell into myself again.

I tired after a minute and sat on the wet concrete. I closed my eyes and breathed deeply. The vibrations throughout my body merged and rose up my spine into a low, rumbling noise that seemed to shoot out the top of my head and hover over me in the sky—then, in space. I was dying. My breath slowed, the trembling faded, and I proceeded to bask in the familiar warmth and stillness of the cough syrup high. After a minute or so, I was calm, but the loud rumble continued. I tilted my head up and opened my eyes. It was just a jet, flying somewhere over the clouds.

I quietly stepped back inside the house without waking Faustina and got back in the hammock. I thought of going home and seeing a doctor, but nothing had come of it the last time I'd done that, after my legs had gone into convulsions.

I remember sitting on an examination table at a walk-in clinic. An older doctor questioned me, taking notes.

"Any head injury?"

"No."

"Alcoholism?"

"No."

He looked into my eyes with his scope. "Anything unusual happen in your life lately?"

"No." How could I tell this guy my entire life was out of the ordinary?

He stepped back, crossed his arms. "Everything okay at work?"

I was unemployed. "Yeah, everything's fine."

"Healthy social life, friends, girlfriend?"

I faked a smile. "Yes. Everything is fine, Doc. Am I sick? Is there something wrong with my brain?"

"It sounds like a partial seizure, or a motor attack. We'll send you for a CT scan, to be safe. Just get plenty of rest and you'll be okay."

Now, back in the hammock, I tried to fall asleep, and wondered how many times Faustina had gotten trashed on cough syrup. Maybe her mother checked her into an institution because she'd caught her in the yard, out of her skull and doing jumping jacks.

A noise came from the kitchen. I approached the odd squeaking and spotted a giant rat on the stove. Without hesitating, I grabbed a can of insecticide from the counter and hurled it across the room, missing the rat and shattering the window behind the stove.

The shrill of broken glass woke Faustina, and she shouted, "What was that?"

"A rat. I took care of it."

•

The next morning, Faustina found me sweeping and picking shards out of the *lavadero* outside.

"Did you break the window?" Her voice had a tone I'd never heard from her—a tone that said even though she was eighteen, I was the irresponsible one.

"I was trying to hit the rat."

She hurried outside to tear down her tent. "We'd better get out of here."

I packed my sleeping bag and followed her out. "David," she said without looking at me. "My dad sent me money to take a bus home."

I felt immediate relief, knowing I wouldn't have to keep hitchhiking with her—to feel responsible or guilty of anything.

●

We lugged our backpacks to the plaza and ate breakfast on the sidewalk—stale *conchas* and a box of orange juice from a corner store. Afterwards, we walked to the bus station without a word, and split the weed.

"If you come through Guadalajara, will you visit me?" she asked.

"Of course!"

We hugged and said goodbye. She must have known I was lying, because she never gave me her address.

CHAPTER FOURTEEN

I walked out of the city and stopped at a gas station. I was only three hours from Toluca. A young white couple pulled up in a hatchback. While the attendant filled their tank, I approached the driver's door and eyed his empty backseat. "Hey there, if you're going west, would you mind giving me a lift?"

The driver hesitated to answer. He turned to his wife. She held a book and had taken her shoes off, settled in for a long ride. She was smiling politely at me until her husband whispered something to her, and then she stopped smiling. He turned to me and said with a British accent, "We'd rather not."

I stepped aside to let him pay the attendant. "You'd rather not?"

"That's right." He started his car and drove away.

The gas attendant came to me. "He rejected you?"

I felt humiliated. "He's just scared."

"But still, he's your countryman. *Tu paisano.*"

"Not exactly."

•

A beat-up transport pulled up, hissing and rattling and clanking to a stop. The truck looked held together with good luck—the front bumper cracked and duct-taped to the grill. Out came a Mexican driver, around my age, with torn jeans and a black eye.

I met him by the fuel pumps and asked, "You heading toward Toluca?"

"That's where I'm going," he said.

"Could you give me a lift?"

"Of course."

His name was Raimundo. I quickly noticed Raimundo had a twitch—his whole body would jolt, as though he was having a hiccup, but he would simultaneously exhale sharply through his nose.

He had a lengthy, private chat with a gas station attendant. Soon after, a mechanic came out with a giant tire iron and pried a spare tire from the truck.

"What's this about?" I asked.

"I sold it for five hundred pesos. I'll tell my boss it fell off."

"Fell off?"

He simply nodded and went back to his transaction.

With the money, Raimundo bought us *tortas* and *horchatas*, and we ate outside the station at a row of dusty plastic tables with other hungry men.

Raimundo reached into his breast pocket and pulled out some loose pills, dropping two on the table when he twitched.

"What are they?"

"Hielo."

"¿Hielo?"

"*Anfetaminas*. You want some?"

We hit the road wired and leaned over the dashboard with our speeding heads.

"Feels like we're firefighters!" Raimundo said.

But it felt to me like it was the truck that was on fire as it shrieked and slowed to a pathetic uphill crawl.

I smelled burning metal, then I smelled the rain before it came down hard, dousing the windows like fire hoses.

"This stretch of road is dangerous," he said, twitching several times. "Sometimes, at night, they'll have a woman stand on the road. If you pull over for her, men will run out from the woods with machetes."

I stared out into the darkness, searching for men with machetes—like a nightmare I was having of the Mexicans on Bard's farm—fearing the sudden appearance of a lone woman. There was nothing out there, except for visions of having my throat hacked.

•

We entered Mexico City around 3 a.m. The police stopped us on a deserted street, pulling over ahead of the truck.

Raimundo stepped out and approached the driver's side of the car. How many more pills did he have in the truck, I wondered. And what other drugs? How long before his weird spasms prompted them to search the truck? If they found anything, he could pin it on me. Maybe that's why he picked me up, to be his patsy. I thought of running out of the truck and down an alley, but moments later, Raimundo returned and started the truck up again.

The cops drove away.

"What did they want?" I asked.

"Nothing."

"What do you mean, *nothing*?"

"They just checked up."

He shuddered several times in a row, and I knew he'd lied when two blocks later we approached the same police car parked on the centre median, perpendicular to the truck. Raimundo stopped again.

"Where are you going?" I asked.

He slid out of the truck and walked to the car. He leaned on the driver's door. The cop in the passenger seat pulled out a searchlight and shined it at me, blinding me. I closed my eyes and thought of slipping on my sunglasses, but didn't want to look like a smartass, so I just sat there and squeezed my eyes shut like an idiot.

The searchlight eventually turned off, releasing me, and Raimundo's door opened. The cops drove away.

"What did they want?"

"Nothing." He fired the truck up once more and jammed it into gear.

"What did they say?"

"Not much, checking things out."

His caginess irritated me. "Did you pay them off?"

Raimundo shook his head.

"Did they ask about me?"

Nothing.

Moments later, we turned onto an on-ramp and Raimundo slammed his brakes. The ramp was closed.

"Ah, shit." He slapped his steering wheel. "I forgot they closed this."

The setup was obvious. He'd driven me somewhere secluded for the cops to drag me out of the truck, whack me over the head with their batons, and rob me. I searched in the mirror for the cop car. My heart raced. I grabbed my backpack and opened the door.

"What the hell are you doing? Close the door! I gotta back out of here!"

Raimundo started to reverse, so I closed the door, and between spasms, he eased the truck back onto the road. My eyes jumped from Raimundo to the mirror and all around in search of the cops, but nothing happened, and we drove on to Toluca.

CHAPTER FIFTEEN

At the Toluca bus station, I bought a ten-peso calling card and found a payphone with a phone book. I knew Púas' real name was Osvaldo Villafuerte. A hundred Villafuertes were listed. I started at the top, figuring it might not be long before I reached someone related to Púas, but what happened on my first call made my head spin.

"*¿Bueno?*" a man answered.

"*Hola*, I'm trying to find Osvaldo."

"Yes, one minute."

"Hold on. I'm looking for someone they call *El Púas*."

"Yes. That's my son. One moment."

Seconds later, Púas came to the phone. "*¿Bueno?*"

"Púas? It's David, the Canadian!"

"*¡No mames!* Where are you?"

"I'm in Toluca. Are you alright?

"Yeah, why?"

"Antonio told us you were killed!"

•

Waiting for Púas to pick me up, I sat on a bench next to a pretty Mexican woman in a long white dress. Her children, a boy and girl, around three and five years old, sat at her feet and played with toy cars. All three of them had pale skin and clear, blue eyes. The children's innocent little voices echoed through the vast emptiness of the station, while their mother watched over them like a heavenly protector. In another life, we were a family. When I tried to imagine, to remember, the love between the four of us, I felt as frail as a ghost—a young father who had died without saying goodbye. My heart whispered: *I don't want to go anywhere.* I wanted the woman to fall in love with me. But her husband came and took them away.

"*¡Güero!*" Púas shouted across the giant waiting room. He ran to me with an enormous grin and hugged me.

"What happened in Veracruz?" I asked. "Zuriaa thinks you're dead. Antonio told us you got stabbed in an alley."

We walked out of the station toward his father's Chevy Corsa, hopping into the hot car.

"She knows I'm not dead," he said. "I've sent her emails."

It relieved me to know Zuriaa wasn't out there thinking Púas had been murdered.

"Some Colombian guy led us into an alley," he said. "Three guys jumped me, and Antonio ran like a bitch. I got knocked out. After I woke up, I couldn't find you guys, so I took a bus home. I still have your tent. Did you hitchhike here alone?"

"I left Veracruz with that Faustina girl Antonio was always going on about."

"Did you bang her?"

"No. It turned out she was eighteen."

He shook his head. "*Oye*, if you're a homo, it's fine with me, man."

"She's a kid! How old are you?"

"Twenty-two."

"Maybe it's different for you," I said. "But she's too young for me. I'm twenty-five."

"*Eres fresa*," he said. "Anyway, where's Zuriaa? She won't answer my emails."

"She went to Chiapas. I think she's coming home soon."

"Oh yeah? That gives me an idea," he said. "I should get the answer about my work visa application any day now. We're going to need money."

Púas drove us into a neighbourhood called Semenario, where the homes were hidden behind concrete walls, gates, and metal doors. We parked and walked around the corner to a yellow house with barred windows and barking rooftop dogs. Púas reached through the gate and knocked.

A woman opened the door. She wore a tank top and hospital pants. "Púas? You're back in town?"

"We have to talk. Can we come in?"

A worried expression took over her face. She let us in. "When did you arrive?"

"We just got off the bus from Veracruz," he said. "Zuriaa ran off."

I sat quietly, watching him cook up another one of his schemes. The woman shook her head. "Take a seat. I'll get coffee." She shuffled into the kitchen in her slippers. "Who's your friend?"

"This is David from Canada. He speaks Spanish."

"Oh yeah, I heard of you, David," she said from the kitchen.

"You confused, *güero*?" Púas asked.

"Yes."

"That's Zuriaa's mom."

It was hard to believe because she looked to be in her early thirties. She must have had Zuriaa at a young age. She returned from the kitchen with a tray loaded with cinnamon cookies and coffee, lowered her tray onto the coffee table, and sat on the sofa across from us. She looked to Púas. "So she ran off on you?"

"Yup, but I know she's on her way to Guatemala."

"*Guatemala*?" Zuriaa's mother turned to me with concern. "David, I understand you spent a fair amount of time with my daughter. What is your opinion of... her situation?"

I hesitated to answer. "I'm not sure what you mean."

"Did you, for instance, witness her using drugs?"

My eyes wandered to Púas. He wore an oddly pompous smirk. "Be honest, *güero*. Tell her *everything*."

"Sure, she smoked a little pot," I said. "But Zuriaa's not a drug addict."

She sighed. "By the way, my daughter's real name is Cecilia. And *Cecilia* ran away from home. I'm concerned about her."

I couldn't lie to her. "She said she's coming home soon because she wants to go back to school."

She smiled, while Púas squirmed in his chair.

"It'll be nice to have her home," Zuriaa's mother said. Then she stared at me while stirring sugar into her black coffee. "You know, when Cecilia visited, she showed me photos she'd taken of you on a bus. You're not photogenic, *güero*. You're actually quite handsome."

Púas had heard enough. "*Señora*, we have to go."

Zuriaa's mother led us to the door and hugged me on the way out.

In the car, Púas slapped my shoulder. "What did you do that for?"

"Do what?"

"You should have scared the shit out of her."

"Why?"

"She would have paid me to find Zuriaa."

"You told me to be honest."

"Honest?" He almost died laughing. "*¡Te estaba hechando los perros, güero!* You see?"

"She was throwing me dogs? What?"

"She was flirting with you!"

"Oh."

"So, go bang her. I'll wait in the car."

"I'm not going to bang Zuriaa's—*Cecilia's* mom!"

•

Púas opened the door to his mother's place. We entered a living room with pink walls, minimally furnished with old things. Púas handed me my tent as his six-foot-tall mother came out of the kitchen. Púas tossed his arm around my neck and messed my hair. "This is David, the writer who'll get me a job on a farm in Canada. Ma, he's so resourceful—you know how he found our phone number? In a *pinche* phone book!"

•

I slept on a row of couch cushions along Púas' bedroom wall. In the morning, I woke up to a dog barking outside. I thought, only in Latin America do dogs bark this way and everyone sleeps through it. But then Púas shouted, "*¡Cayate!*" and went to his window, opened it, and yelled something else at the dog—something only he and the dog understood. It stopped barking.

I walked over, poked my head out the window, and jumped back when a disfigured white bull terrier leapt up to sniff at me. Its face looked like a Halloween mask—its right eye and a chunk of its nose were missing, and scar tissue covered its left eye.

"What's wrong with it?"

"My brother used to fight him in Mexico City," Púas said. "But it's retired now. Too old. And blind." He grabbed a watch off the floor. "Oh, shit. My girlfriend's coming over soon." He sat up and stretched. "*¿La aventamos el mañanero, juntos?*"

"What does that mean? Smoke a joint?"

"No. It means you can *cojer* her with me."

I tilted my head to gauge his seriousness, and he matched me with a steady gaze as he threw on his pants. "You don't want to get laid, *wey*? It'll never be easier."

"Fucking your girlfriend with you doesn't sound easy to me."

He gave me that look again. "*Are* you *joto*?"

"Gay? No. I wouldn't keep a hard-on with you in the room!"

"Oh, so you're *shy*."

•

Púas stood on his parents' sofa with his head out the window, straining to see beyond the wall. "I can't let her knock on the gate. She'll wake up my mom." Then he hopped off the couch and ran out the door. He came back with a curvy girl who smoked a cigarette and wore too much makeup. He introduced us, and as we shook hands, Púas stood behind her, thrusting his pelvis in the air to entice me. I almost laughed in the poor girl's face.

He sent her to his room. "Are you sure?" he whispered.

"Positive."

"Alright, but if my mother comes downstairs, tell her I'm cleaning my room." He closed the door to his bedroom.

I lay on the sofa with a pen and a dozen pages of my manuscript, but I listened to Púas and his girlfriend tear at each other's clothes and roll around the bed. A few minutes later, his mother came downstairs.

"*Buenos días,*" she said.

"*Buenos días.*"

"Where's Osvaldo?"

"*Esta limpiando su cuarto.*"

She grinned and walked into the kitchen. Púas cracked his bedroom door open, shirtless. I mouthed, "*Tu mamá.*" He closed his door. Seconds later, he led his girlfriend out of the room. They tiptoed toward the door. Púas opened the door, careful not to make it creak, and his girlfriend walked away.

From the kitchen, his mother said, "She could have stayed for breakfast."

•

I showered with cool water, and thought of warm showers and baths, and wondered if Púas' mother had ever had a warm bath in her life. Later, I sat at the kitchen table alone with her. She said Púas had run out for a minute. We ate eggs, beans, and tortillas, and chatted about how she hoped I could help Púas find work in Canada and make a life for himself.

"You don't think he's too much of a troublemaker to enter your country, do you?"

I laughed nervously.

Suddenly, Púas barged in and dragged three garbage bags across the floor.

"What are those? Where were you?" his mother asked.

Púas tossed the bags in his room. "I picked up my clothes."

"Did you *pay* Alma?"

"No." He sat at the table and fixed himself a plate.

"She *gave* them to you?"

"No. I waited for her to leave her store, like she always does, and I went behind the counter and got them myself."

His mother dropped her fork. "¿*Que?*"

Púas avoided looking at his mother. "I need a full wardrobe. David and I have to dress up a little and go out—meet some women." He winked at me.

Púas' mother shook her head. "Don't get yourself into trouble again. What if they don't let you into Canada? Isn't that right, David?"

All I could do was shrug.

•

In the bedroom, Púas tore the garbage bags open and spread his perfectly folded clothes onto the bed.

He sniffed a wool sweater. "Alma used to clean my clothes for free. We had an arrangement. You see how tight it's all folded? You'd think they use a machine, but no. This is hand-folded."

"What do you mean, an *arrangement*?"

"She did my laundry, and I banged her. That was the deal."

I laughed. "You're like a prostitute!"

"Romy—my girlfriend—works at a restaurant. I have breakfast there on weekends, for free. The problem is, Alma got pissed when I bailed for Oaxaca. When I came back for my clothes last week, she said I owed her four hundred pesos. Can you imagine? I wouldn't have left so much clothing with her if I had to pay for it!"

He picked a pair of jeans and a shirt and tossed them to me. "Here, don't wear your rags while you're here." I tried his clothes on and they fit. "Now maybe we can find a girl to keep you around a while." He closed his door and whispered, "I need you to go to the laundromat in a bit and lure Alma outside... I know where she keeps their cash box."

"How am I supposed to do that?"

"Charm her. Tell her you're from Canada. Take her for a walk around the block."

He stood and looked ready to move forward with his plan.

"Won't it be obvious who robbed her?" I asked. "You took your clothes from her an hour ago—what if she's already noticed it's gone? And won't she think it's odd if people see you around town with some Canadian guy?"

I must have looked nervous, because Púas put his hand on my shoulder. "*Güero*, I can tell you're an artist! You're so sensitive. But you're right. It's too obvious, *wey*. I'll go alone." He pulled a clean shirt off the bed. "Goddamn, look how clean this shirt is! This was full of bloodstains."

•

I worked on my pages, worried when I heard Púas' mother sweeping the floor outside the room. If she came into the room, she'd ask where he had gone. I didn't want to see the disappointed look on her face. I lay on the cushions and pretended to sleep.

Ten minutes later, the front door crashed open. Púas ran into the house.

"Hey," his mother shouted. "Take off your shoes. I just swept in here!"

He ignored her, barged into the room, and slammed the door shut. Out of breath, he collapsed on the bed and laughed his ass off. He shoved his hand in his pants, fished out a handful of cash, and spread it over his bed. He counted and organized his loot. "Look, a fake two hundred!" he shouted, studying the bill. "This is a quality forgery." He slipped the money under his mattress and ran to the washroom.

His mother stood with her broom in her hand, her eyes fixed on the floor. She must have known what her son had done.

•

In the evening, Púas and I went out for tacos.

"What did your mom mean about you getting into trouble again?" I asked.

"I did a few months in jail a couple of years ago. I got kicked off the Olympic trials because of it."

"Why were you in jail?"

Púas sounded almost apologetic when he explained, "My friend and I robbed a house one night... The owner came downstairs—we didn't think she was home—so we tied her up with her belts and gagged her, just to keep her quiet. We loaded her minivan with her stuff and drove to Mexico City to sell it all. That's where the cops busted us."

"Maybe you should write about your life," I said.

"*Güero*, nobody wants to read about shit like that."

"I do."

•

When we got back to his house, his mother stormed out of the kitchen. "The police came for you!"

she said. "I had to lie and tell them you were still in Oaxaca."

I kept walking and hid in the bedroom.

"I did nothing wrong, Ma!"

"Don't lie to me! I know what you did."

"If she's *pendeja* enough to leave her business unattended, that's her problem!"

"You don't leave this house until this blows over. If you leave, don't come back!"

Púas stormed into his bedroom and swung a crazy right hook into his door, slamming it shut.

•

I stayed with Púas and his mother for a week, finishing revisions and helping Púas' mother by running errands, while Púas mostly stayed home to avoid being seen. After breakfast, I would head to an internet café, and in three days, I typed up my new draft of *Curriculum Vitae*. It had settled into a svelte one-hundred-page novella. On March 13, two days before our agreed-upon deadline, I emailed the story to Bella Chevalier. I tossed my printed manuscript in the trash, then bought fresh tortillas and cheese, and entered Púas' house with a giant smile.

He stood in the living room, shadowboxing and sweaty.

"My Canadian work visa got rejected, *güero*. They said I can't enter Canada because of my criminal record!"

The news didn't surprise me. I didn't know what to say. I didn't want to tell him I'd submitted *Curriculum Vitae*.

He sat on the sofa and let out a loud sigh, surrendering. "What are you going to do, *güero*, head up to your friend's farm?"

"Yeah," I said. "It might be time for me to leave."

I thought of an email I'd received a week earlier from Paul Orr—the auctioneer who I worked with in Toronto. Paul had written that he was flying into Puerto Vallarta and asked if I'd be anywhere near there. I hadn't thought of it at the time, but now with no money to make it to Mazatlán, I responded to Paul's email and told him I'd see him soon. Paul was loaded; he could easily afford to loan me a hundred bucks.

CHAPTER SIXTEEN

Two rides took me away from Toluca. Late afternoon, I walked Highway 15 outside Puertas del Tule and found a rig pulled over on the shoulder. The driver stood on his front tire, his torso buried under the hood.

"Excuse me?"

"*¿Sí?*" the big man said. He had a front tooth missing, and a giant, warped head.

"Are you going toward Puerto Vallarta?" I asked.

"That's where I'm going. I'm about ready to go. You need a lift?"

"*Sí.*"

We took off and talked about my travels until the sun went down, but when I tried to sleep, so I could arrive in Vallarta fresh and ready to meet up with Paul and discuss my loan, Nacho—the driver—prodded me with questions.

"So, what's the money in Central America?" he asked.

"The money?"

"Yeah, what does it look like? What do the coins look like?"

I kept my head resting against the window. "I'm not sure. I have one or two in my bag. I'll give you one in Vallarta."

"What are the women like in Costa Rica?"

"Huh?"

"The women. What do they look like? You said you passed through Nicaragua, too. How do they look down *there*? I heard they all have huge tits!"

"I didn't notice."

"You fuck any of them?"

"No."

I closed my eyes, hoping he'd stop talking.

"How about El Salvadorian women? Are they all sluts?"

I kept my eyes shut. "I didn't sleep with any Central American women."

"No? Oh, hey. It's none of my business, but are you gay?"

"Why does everyone down here think I'm gay if I don't sleep with every woman I can? Anyway, I slept with a Canadian girl in Costa Rica. Violet. Violeta."

"Oh, so you're not gay?"

"No."

•

At night, I awoke in the dark cab. We were on our descent from the mountains, and in the distance, the trees of the southern Sierra Madre stopped and the cold buildings of Puerto Vallarta began. Driving by a gas station, we passed a clock that read 2 a.m., then we entered an undeveloped resort area along the beach and drove down a long street stabbed with palm trees—no streetlights.

Nacho pulled over. "Here we are."

"Here?"

"I haul materials for the new hotel over there." He pointed into the darkness. Beside us were empty lots with partial hotel frames, locked up behind construction fencing and lit only by moonlight.

Nacho pulled out a warm six-pack from under his seat. "You want a beer?"

"No, thanks." I was looking for a place to go, searching up and down the street. "I guess I'll go pitch my tent in one of these empty lots."

"You can sleep in the bed," he said, as he opened his door and went outside. "I'm going to sit by the gate and wait for the guard to let me in at six."

Nacho walked to the gate, sat on a cinder block, and cracked open a beer. I kicked my shoes off and crawled between the seats and onto the little bed. My body crumpled in surrender. Within seconds, I could hear myself snoring.

The driver door swung open and woke me.

"You sure you don't want a beer?" Nacho asked. I pretended to sleep, but the truck jostled and I opened my eyes a slit. He climbed into bed, shirtless. "Too many mosquitos."

He lay with his back to me. I tried to ignore the stink of his armpits and fall asleep again, but he squirmed and whined. "They chewed me alive." Then he pushed up against my shoulder and rubbed himself against me. My eyes sprang open, and I sat up with my fist clenched, ready to bash his face in if he came at me again.

"What's wrong?" he asked, as I climbed over him and into the passenger seat. "You don't want to sleep in the bed?"

"No. It's too hot."

I fished my flimsy steak knife out of my bag, imagining Nacho wrapping a wire around my neck. I slipped my shoes on, prepared to run into the darkness and hide, but he lay still and quiet and began snoring.

I couldn't sleep. I felt like a paranoid homophobe, but was also disgusted with Nacho for luring and cornering me in his bed. I thought about what I would have done if Nacho had attacked me and I'd killed him: Search for money, then set the cab on fire and run.

Waiting for sunrise, I watched the sky for hours. I hadn't slept in two nights. My whole face hurt.

Eventually the black sky gave way to a crisp blue dawn, and I slipped out of the truck and pulled my bag down. Nacho rolled over.

"You're leaving already?" he asked.

"I want to start walking before it gets too hot." I swung my bag on—one hand on the door.

"Wait!" he cried. "What about the coins?" He poked his weird head and dishevelled hair out from between the seats.

I dropped my bag on the sidewalk and searched through a pocket, desperate to uncover any old coin to amuse him. I found one and handed it to him.

"What is it?"

"It's Costa Rican—twenty colones."

He studied the coin. "How much is it worth?"

"About five dollars," I lied. "Thanks for the ride."

•

I strode toward sunrise along a white sidewalk for an hour, passing construction sites on the beach: concrete frames, holes, and heaps of dirt—a once-stunning panorama, now excavated, disemboweled and exhumed. Finally I arrived at the resorts. They were the first resorts I'd ever seen—synthetic, fishbowl landscapes complete with castles and palm trees.

A cab pulled up, and two American frat boys stumbled out. They spotted me right away. They were red-eyed and smelled like beer.

"Hey, man, you have any rolling papers?" the taller one asked.

"Sure." I started to take off my bag, eager to befriend the guys and hoping they would let me sleep on the floor of their room.

"No, no. Not here," he said. "You want to burn one with us?"

"Of course."

The taller one was Jake. I followed him and Mikey, his chubby sidekick, through a narrow path beside their hotel, on a pruned and sterile walkway. I expected someone to throw me off the property very soon.

Jake stopped before we stepped onto the beach. "Mikey, give him your sweater; the guards won't see he doesn't have a wristband."

They showed me their orange wristbands—proof they were guests. Mikey tore off his sweater. I put on the grey UCF sweater, which was much too big for me; I felt embarrassed looking like a college boy.

"I'll carry your bag," Mikey said. "I've never carried a huge backpack before."

Mikey struggled to swing it onto his back. "How the hell do you do this?" Jake had to help him fit the straps over his shoulders, but when he leaned forward to hike the bag up his back, the weight of it bent him forward until the bag slid up his back and fell to the ground. He stood there folded over until Jake picked him up.

On the beach, I took off my shoes and walked through the hot sand. I wandered away from Jake and Mikey, drawn toward the water. On the harder sand, tiny crabs scurried into their holes. I soaked my feet in the ocean and let the cool waves come up to my knees.

At the end of a long pier, we climbed the rail and sat on the rocks, hidden from the beach. Mikey rolled a fat joint with the papers I handed him. He sparked it up and handed me the small *tubo*.

"You can take the rest of this," he said. "Our flight's in four hours."

I took the *tubo* happily, but the news they were leaving crushed me.

"How long have you been travelling?" Mikey asked.

"About four months." I took the joint when Mikey offered it to me.

Jake slapped his knee. "Damn! Mikey, if I weren't in college, I'd do what he's doing."

I shrugged. "So drop out and travel."

"Drop out?"

They had a good laugh.

I kept smoking. These guys *would* stay in school, I thought. They were good boys. They'd graduate, start a long career, and handcuff themselves to a soft couch in front of a big TV.

We jolted when half a dozen dolphins began vaulting out of the ocean. Their sparkling leaps and dives surrounded the end of the pier. We stood, spellbound and slightly alarmed.

"What is happening?" Mikey asked.

"A tsunami... maybe an earthquake," Jake said.

"No. It's some sort of sign," Mikey said. "This is some sort of phenomenon."

An object flew from behind me.

I spun around and saw an old woman on the pier, flinging pieces of bread into the water. A couple of other tourists hurried down the pier to feed the dolphins, too.

I tore Mikey's sweater off and handed it to him. "I'm taking off. This place is just a goddamned zoo."

CHAPTER SEVENTEEN

In Old Vallarta, I splurged on a fifty-peso breakfast of *chilaquiles* with coffee. Little by little, the waking tourists wandered the sidewalks, everyone from hungover college kids to leathery, old snowbirds. By 9 a.m., I wandered down Boulevard Malecón. The shops had opened and spilled their bright colours and plastic and leather souvenirs onto the sidewalk. I looked homeless—days without a shower and sleep, my crazy hair all over the place—but still, at every turn, someone hassled me in English, assuming I had money. "Hey man, you want cigars?" "Taxi?" "Tattoos?" "Come on inside, *amigo*, we have souvenirs, towels, T-shirts."

"*No, gracias*," I said repeatedly, refusing to answer anyone in English. "*No. Gracias.*"

In an internet cafe, I read an email from Paul. He had arrived the night before. His room wasn't far from the cafe. He wanted to meet at 11 p.m. at the Barrio Vallarta, a bar on Calle Francisco I. Madero.

I drifted through twisted little streets and friendly faces, climbing the hills away from the tourist trap, into what felt more like Mexico to me.

Alongside a narrow dirt road, a slow river meandered its way toward the ocean. I stopped in the shade under trees with drooping vines and enjoyed a cool breeze. At a *tienda*, I bought a bottle of water. I had noticed a washboard and clothesline outside, under a corrugated metal roof. I asked the woman if I could wash my clothes outside.

"Yes, of course! Help yourself."
"Is it safe to swim in the river?"
"My kids swim there every day!"

I washed every piece of clothing and even my backpack, hung it all on the clothesline, and then headed down to the river in my swim shorts.

Upstream, a big rock sat out in the middle of the water. I swam to the rock with a joint in my mouth and lay there for hours. I basked in the sun like a seal, occasionally throwing myself in the water to cool off. Strangers walked by the riverside. Kids swam in the water. I smiled and said *hola* to everyone who looked at me, hoping someone might take an interest in me—but when no one did, it didn't matter. I closed my eyes and waited for my clothes to dry. Downstream, someone whistled *La Llorona*. I felt so alive.

•

With a fresh plaid shirt and shorts, I strolled down to the Barrio Vallarta around 10 p.m. I poked my head inside the bar to look for Paul. I pushed my way through a drunken dance party—a crowd of white twentysomethings—but no sign of Paul yet. I sat on a bench outside and ate tacos I'd bought from a street vendor—one *asada*, one *al pastor*, and one *chorizo*, and loaded them with everything they had: guacamole, beans, onions, turnips, cilantro, and hot salsa. I sat on the bench and read Dostoevsky's *Notes from Underground* while a steady stream of obnoxious young tourists poured into the bar shouting drunk nonsense. I ordered another *chorizo* taco and a bottle of water. I had two hundred and twenty pesos left.

But 11 p.m. came and went and, still, there was no sign of Paul.

Around midnight, I locked eyes with a tall, blue-eyed blonde who walked with a friend. She flashed a big, beautiful smile at me, and pain stabbed my chest when they walked away—how pathetic I must have looked camped out on that bench. I got up, ready to head up to my river spot, and cursed Paul for deserting me.

"Excuse me," a female voice said. The blonde had come back. She sat on the bench with me and we introduced ourselves.

"I'm Laura. You look like you need a place to stay."

"I do. I planned to meet a friend at 11, but he didn't show."

"Did you just get into town?"

"Yeah. I hitchhiked from Costa Rica."

"That's quite a trek." Laura pulled a pen and notepad from her bag. "If you don't find your friend, you're welcome to stay at our place."

"Thank you."

"It's not a problem. I've been in your shoes before." Laura placed her notepad on her thighs and began to draw a map. She was rescuing me. I tried not to stare at her thighs poking out from under her dress.

She tore the page out of her notebook and handed it to me. "This is a little bridge right here." She pointed.

"Looks like a tourist map," I said.

"Well, I guess that's what it is."

"Thank you. I appreciate it."

"I should get back to my friend. I hope you find *your* friend."

•

I walked into the bar to have one last look for Paul. The place was overrun. I was wondering why so many young people had come to Puerto Vallarta, when it occurred to me it was spring break. There I was with my big, dumb backpack, like I'd crashed a college movie scene, and at any moment, someone would yell, "Cut!" and they'd yank me off the set.

I spotted Paul seated alone at the bar. With his pasty bald head and new Acapulco shirt, he looked more out of place than me.

Paul shouted when he saw me. "Holy shit, look at that huge bag! How are ya? You look so skinny! Want a beer?"

"Sure."

Paul signalled the bartender for two *cervezas*. He dropped fifty pesos on the bar and only got back ten pesos.

"Did he charge you *twenty* pesos a beer?"

"Yeah! Two bucks... Crazy, huh? You got the next round!" He was in stitches over how cheap the drinks and food and cab were in Mexico, even though the prices were triple what we would have paid away from the tourist areas. "So, what have you been doing in Mexico?"

I thought this might steer our conversation to my financial situation. "I've done a lot of hitchhiking."

"Hitchhiking? No way. You're crazy!"

"Maybe I am," I said, almost building up the nerve to ask him for a loan.

"Well, drink up! Hey, what are your plans tomorrow? You should come with us. I met some people on the plane. We're scuba diving with dolphins—only a hundred and forty bucks—can you imagine? Dolphins!"

A hundred and forty bucks? I'd survive two months here on a hundred and forty bucks.

I paid for the next round, then Paul bought the third round, and I had to sit through shop talk and his general assumption that I was on a regular holiday, not homeless.

"Hey, you want a shot?" We threw down shots of tequila. "Where are you staying, anyway?"

"I'm still looking for a place."

"Well, shit. Get a room at my hotel! It's right on the beach. Eighty bucks a night." He slapped my shoulder.

Looking into his excited face—the face of a man on vacation and free of concern—I lost the courage to ask him for money. After all, I hardly knew Paul; we'd only worked together for six months—gotten drunk together once or twice. It was ridiculous of me to have even thought of asking.

I got up before he had me pay another round. "Earlier, I met an American girl on the street. She offered to let me crash at her place."

"You dog!"

"I should get going. I can't show up drunk."

Paul followed me out of the bar. We walked in opposite directions. At first, he didn't notice. "Oh, you're going *that* way?" He chased after me and handed me a card from his hotel with his room number written on it.

"Call me tomorrow. We'll do the diving tour!"

"Sure thing!" I waved goodbye and turned up a quiet street to get away. I heard Paul shout, "Fucking dolphins, Dave!"

"It's David!"

I flung his card in a trash can.

•

I attempted to follow Laura's map, but when I came to the bridge that crossed Isla Cuale for the second time, I was lost. A cigarette ember burned in the dark—a prostitute leaned on a column at the end of the bridge.

I approached her and held out Laura's map. "*¿Disculpe, podrías echarme una mano con estas instrucciones?*"

She sucked on her cigarette, rolled her head toward me, and sighed. "I can't help you."

I held the map closer. "My friend drew me a map. Do you recognize this street name? *Aguales*? I can't read it."

Now she spoke English. "I *wone* help you. Go *ass* a *tassi* driver."

I responded in Spanish. "In this tourist trap? A cab driver won't offer me directions here—he'd take me for a ride."

She turned away.

I walked up to a taco stand instead and showed my map to some locals eating there. Finally, someone told me there were two bridges—and I'd crossed the wrong one. They pointed me in the right direction.

I climbed through the cobbled neighbourhood, up steep concrete stairs until I found the house. I pushed open a short, metal gate and stepped onto a patio. The house lights were out. I thought I might wake someone if I knocked, so I walked onto the neighbour's flat roof, where I yanked out my sleeping bag, kicked off my shoes, and smiled at a sky flooded with stars.

•

"Buenos días."

I opened my eyes to see Laura hovering over me, clutching her fluffy white housecoat closed against the cool morning.

Looking up at her friendly face, I said, "Sorry about sleeping here. I didn't want to wake anyone last night."

"I thought you might end up out here. Glad you found the place. You want to come inside? I made coffee."

I followed Laura into the kitchen of her sparsely furnished adobe home. Laura sat at the table, where her cup of coffee waited. "Help yourself to some toast and peanut butter."

"Thanks." I dropped a slice of bread in the toaster.

"Did you find your friend last night?" she asked.

"No. He must have missed his flight." I couldn't tell her the ugly truth—that I hardly knew Paul and had only met with him to borrow money.

"Too bad. Maybe you'll meet up with him later."

"I hope so."

I smeared a good chunk of peanut butter on my toast, sat across the table from Laura, and sipped the black coffee she'd poured for me.

"Where are you from?" she asked.

"Canada."

"I thought I heard an accent."

"Where are *you* from?"

"I'm from Nashville, but I study Latin American politics in Portland. It's my reading week... I'm kind of housesitting. The house was my father's. He died a couple of weeks ago."

"I'm sorry. What happened?"

"Cancer."

"My father died of cancer, too," I said, realizing he had died around this time in March. "What's the date today?" I asked.

"The sixteenth."

The anniversary of my father's death. Tell her, I thought. No. It's too creepy.

"Morning, sunshine!" Laura called out, as a woman with short, wavy red hair entered the kitchen. She was the woman I'd seen Laura walking with the previous night. "Megan, this is Michael."

"David," I said.

Megan gave a half smile. "Hi." She sleepwalked to the coffee pot, poured herself a cup, then walked away.

Laura sighed. "Megan is an old friend of mine from Nashville. She's just tired."

"I'd be disappointed to find a homeless guy in my kitchen," I said, standing beside my backpack, which held every damned thing I owned—a humiliating display of my disastrous life. "Weren't you worried about inviting someone in off the street?"

"You don't look like the serial killer type. Megan was a little worried. She's visiting from New York—first time we've seen each other in six years. We used to be two peas in a pod. We're going to the beach today. You wanna come?"

•

We hit the highway in a convertible Volkswagen Bug with the top down, the girls in the front. Laura wore a green sundress, flip-flops, and sunglasses. I sat in the backseat in my swim trunks—my hair blowing in the wind and whipping my face—unable to hear the girls' conversation. I stole glances at Laura's high cheekbones and broad smile in the rearview mirror. Behind her glasses, I wondered, was she looking at me looking at her?

The car slowed for a *Federales* checkpoint crossing into Nayarit State. When the men took a long, greasy look at the girls, a feeling of pride washed over me because I knew they would think I must have had it all together to wind up in a car with these ladies. Yes, boys, take a good look, I thought. These women know me. And I know them. The blonde? That's my fiancée!

We drove to an empty beach and laid our towels in the shade under a grass hut, where the sand didn't burn. Laura pulled off her dress and revealed a black bikini. She put on a floppy hat and leaned back. She looked like a model in a travel magazine.

Indiscernible white tattoos climbed up her rib cage, and a black one on her shoulder caught my eye: a plain 76.

"What does the 76 mean?" I asked.

She looked at her tattoo as if she'd forgotten it was there. "I got that done with four friends of mine. We were all born in '76."

I showed her the traces of a small tattoo on my shoulder, an embarrassing unity symbol I'd shared with four friends, until I'd had it covered up with Hunter S. Thompson's Gonzo logo. "I had that one done with four friends of mine, too. I was also born in '76."

"You're *my* age? Wow, we thought you were *much* younger."

Megan nodded.

What did that mean—that they thought I should have it together by now?

When Megan took off to buy us a six-pack, Laura and I swam in the ocean. We dove under a wave and then treaded water.

"Laura, last night you said you'd been in my shoes before. What did you mean?"

"When I was seventeen, my boyfriend committed suicide. I ran away from home and came to Mexico... I wound up in San Pancho, close to here. I was tanning on an empty beach one day when this husky voice said, 'Nice tattoos.' Scared the shit out of me. But he turned out to be a nice gay man named Bill. We spent two weeks together and explored beaches and villages. Bill told me that three months before, he was sitting at a bar when he looked up at the TV and saw his boyfriend marrying another man. 'First televised gay marriage in America,' he said. Anyway, two weeks after I'd met him, Bill and I were camped on an island, and he got sick and ran a crazy fever, so I brought him to a doctor in the village. They laid him on a cot, and he fainted right away. He stayed unconscious for three days. At one point, I rummaged around in his bag. I thought maybe he needed medication, and that's when I discovered the same drugs my older sister took before she died of AIDS."

"Your boyfriend committed suicide *and* your sister died of AIDS?"

"It's okay. It was years ago."

The waves crashed over us, tossing and twirling us like seaweeds. It was impossible not to smile, impossible not to dream of living here with Laura—being with a woman who could maybe understand me.

•

I stayed at Laura's for a week or so. She'd offered her sofa, but I preferred to sleep in the garden in my sleeping bag. Looking up at the black sky, I sometimes wondered if before he died, her father had held her hand, hugged her, cried with her. Had he spoken to her—left her with wonderful words to cherish as she carried on with the rest of her life?

•

I made myself scarce most days, ate a fresh fruit or a cheap taco, and wandered the narrow streets, stoned out of my head. In Old Vallarta, neighbourhoods had been dug into the mountain where the dogs and children ran around, and little boys would jump out from behind a car, point a toy gun at me, and shout, "¡Arriba las manos!"

I ended my days waiting for sunsets and writing at the lookout point, El Mirador de la Cruz. On my way up to the *mirador* one evening, I checked my email and found a message from Bella Chevalier. I nearly screamed with joy. Attached were my marked-up manuscript, along with a three-page editorial letter.

> *Dear Dave,*
> *Thank you for your novella.*
> *I'm rather fond of your* Curriculum Vitae *idea, and even your protagonist and the little random encounters at his various places of work, which evoke his wandering, but you need to ask yourself why, somewhere inside, there is fear and resistance to what he needs, why he'd rather intoxicate himself and cut and run, than feel vulnerable.*

I scrolled through the pages but quickly stopped. She had ravaged every page of the story with red strikethroughs and black notes. It looked vandalized, condemned. I would need years on Ignacio's farm to make sense of it all. I was too ashamed to even respond to her.

Sitting atop the *mirador*, I felt the empty, gutless sensation of inadequacy and a colossal loneliness as I overlooked rivers and roads, rooftops, poles, and power lines—all sloping toward the rippling, endless ocean and its crushing scope. I smoked the last of my weed with notepad in hand, and wrote nothing.

•

One night, Laura asked me to join her and Megan for dinner at a restaurant in Old Vallarta.

There wasn't a single Mexican customer in the place—the waiter even spoke to me in English. I ordered three tacos for fifty pesos—the cheapest thing on the menu. I had a hundred and thirty pesos left, and no idea when or how I'd make it to Mazatlán. I began to sweat and there was no hiding it—I could feel the drops running down my face. I was melting in my chair. I needed cold water, but my hands trembled so much, I was afraid to reach for the glass—afraid I'd drop it or choke on the water and make an ass of myself. Would I swallow my tongue—have a seizure? A shiver grabbed hold of me and wouldn't let go. The restaurant voices grew. Everyone was shouting. A rage fomented inside of me. I needed silence. The surrounding laughter seemed to ridicule me, and I was trapped in my head, unable to hear anything Laura and Megan were saying.

"Why is it so hot in here?" I asked.

Laura grabbed my arm. "Try to relax. I think you're having culture shock." Her voice eased my tension. "You'll have to teach me some Spanish, David."

Teach her Spanish? I thought. Did she want me to stay?

Walking back to Laura's, I observed the procession of tourists and wondered if I could live here and tolerate them for a while. I listened to their English, and decided they were mostly Americans and Canadians. If I came up with a story about how a trucker had stolen my wallet and passport—that I couldn't fly home—I could conjure some sympathy, maybe wrangle some money. How hard could it be? On the way back to Laura's, I schemed. With no guitar or drums, what else could I do? So it was settled.

•

Later that evening, Laura and I drank a cold beer in the garden while Megan showered.

Laura asked, "When did your father die?"

"It was actually seven years ago, the day I got here."

"That's crazy! What type of cancer?"

"Pancreatic. What about your dad?"

"Prostate... He started feeling pain when we hiked—" Her eyes welled up. "Sorry, I don't want to break down."

We were shipwrecked, and had drifted into each other's lives, buoyed by coincidence—yet I couldn't even offer an uplifting word. I could only think of running away. "Let's not talk about it."

After Laura went to sleep, Megan came out to the garden.

"Dave, we enjoy having you around," she said. "But do you know when you'll leave?"

"Not really."

"Thing is, I flew here from New York when I heard Laura's father passed. And we'd like to spend time alone together, you know? It's kind of a girlfriend thing."

I wondered if Laura knew about this conversation—or if perhaps she'd put Megan up to it. Either way, at that moment, I felt like a cockroach—stomped upon and soon to be swept outside. I began to think Megan had poisoned Laura with suspicions that I had lied about the anniversary of my father's death or sharing the same tattoo with four friends. I hadn't even told her that my ex's name was Laura. Or about my uncle's suicide. It was all too much. It sounded like bad fiction, and I shouldn't have told Laura about any of it.

"I'll leave tomorrow," I said.

Megan looked surprised, and with a hint of pity in her voice, she asked, "Where will you go?"

"North."

"Hitchhiking?"

"Yes."

"Can you call home for someone to help you?"

"No, there's no one."

"You don't have a family?"

"Just my mother and younger sister."

"Can your mom help?"

"No. She's not working... She's disabled from a stroke she had a couple of years ago."

"That's awful. Maybe it would be good for you to go home and help her."

My eyes narrowed at the smart look on her face. What did she know about my mother? She didn't know my mother's sister lived up the street, and that my sister lived across the street. Go home and help her? She had enough help. She was fine.

After Megan left, I stretched out on my sleeping bag and remembered my mother in the quietness of her hospital room after her stroke, struggling to spell words with block letters, legs tucked tight under a white blanket. When she saw me, her eyes opened wider than I'd ever seen them, and she gasped, "David." Someone said the stroke had paralyzed her right arm, so I took her left hand, dropped my head on her belly, and cried.

"I'm not going anywhere," she said.

I didn't believe her.

"I plan to stick around for a while," she said. "Stir shit around a little bit."

It was such an odd thing for her to say that I started laughing. Then she laughed. Then I was pretending to laugh, but I was crying.

•

I woke before sunrise, and felt the urge to start my journey to Mazatlán before Laura came downstairs and made my shame real again. I packed my backpack, wrote the girls a thank you note, and stole a slice of bread. Stuck on the refrigerator was a yellowed paper with a typewritten quote. I scribbled the quote in my notepad, but didn't know why I wanted to remember it:

> *He was free, but too infinitely free; not striding upon the earth but floating above it. He felt the lack in him of that weight of human relations that trammels a man's progress; tears, farewells, reproaches, joys—all those*

> *things that a man caresses or rips apart each time he sketches a gesture; those thousand ties that bind him to others and lend density to his being.* — Antoine de Saint-Exupéry

The streets were dead. It was too early for tourists. I thought of walking downtown, to wait for the crowds and try my luck at supplication, but the prospect of looking people in the eye and bullshitting them gave me butterflies. I couldn't do it. I needed to get out of town and away from the embarrassment.

CHAPTER EIGHTEEN

I camped at a riverbank near La Higuerita Vieja. The next morning, I walked thirty-six kilometres on an empty stomach until I reached a gas station. I sat on a concrete divider, with my thumb stuck out at a steady stream of tourists, who all drove by and ignored me. I was starving, dehydrated, light-headed, and out of weed. I was warming up to the thought of dying a failure—of accomplishing nothing with my life, as if it didn't matter at all.

"Want a sandwich?" asked a voice behind me. A white man in his sixties. He had white hair, worn-out flip-flops, and blue knee-high socks.

I slid off the divider to join him as he flip-flopped toward a red van. A younger woman with big sunglasses and a green fedora stood outside the sliding side door, making tuna sandwiches. They introduced themselves as Ed and Elena. Ed was from Arizona, and Elena, his forty-something-year-old girlfriend, was from Spain. She handed me a sandwich, and I devoured it like a street dog.

"Where you coming from, kiddo?" Ed asked.

"I started in Costa Rica. Heading to Mazatlán, I think."

"Wow!" Elena said.

"Well," Ed said. "We're going to Mazatlán today, on our way to Tucson. You want a lift?"

"If you don't mind."

"Not at all," Ed said. "You look like the dogs have been keeping you under the porch."

•

The van was carpeted in red and had a backseat big enough for me to stretch out on. When we drove off, wind poured through the windows and dried my sweaty hair.

"Where are you from?" Elena asked.

"Canada."

Ed looked through the rear-view. "We were just talking about Canadians. I wondered if Canadians think more like Europeans than Americans. You know the biggest difference between Americans and Europeans? We Americans have a hard time accepting that other people differ from us. When Americans travel to Europe, we can't accept there's a door that separates the toilet from the rest of our hotel restroom. It's the type of thing we'll tell our friends about when we get home."

"What do you think, David?" Elena asked. "Does that apply to Canadians?"

"I wouldn't talk about a door in the restroom, no."

"Oh!" Elena said. "I know one thing about Canadians." She turned to Ed. "Canadians like picnics."

"Yes, I've heard that about Canadians," he said.

"Picnics?" I asked.

After a silent moment, Elena said, "Will we stop for a picnic to show him, or what, Ed?"

"Already?" Ed said. "We had a picnic half an hour ago."

"But David hasn't had a picnic."

"Alright," Ed said. "Let's see if we can find a nice tree."

Once he found a suitable spot, Ed pulled the van over, and we piled out of it. I looked up at the dusty old tree and found nothing special about it. Ed came over and pulled an Altoids tin out of his pocket. He opened the tin and revealed a dozen joints.

I started laughing. "I thought you guys were actually having a picnic."

Elena lit a joint and handed it over.

"How did you wind up hitchhiking in Mexico?" she asked. "Couldn't you call home for money?"

"No," I said.

"You'd have to be crazy to hitchhike as much as you have. You're not crazy, are you?" She tilted her head back.

"He just wanted an adventure," Ed said.

Elena rolled her eyes. "It's dangerous."

Ed shrugged. "Most adventures are. But sometimes, you just have to paint your butt white and run with the antelope."

"What is this saying?" she said. "Sometimes I think you make them up."

"It means you have to do what you're told," Ed said.

"What do you mean? What told him to hitchhike?"

Ed chuckled. "Who knows? Something did."

And on and on they went, talking about me as if I weren't there.

"Aren't you afraid?" Elena asked.

"Not at all," I said. And I thought, what's the sense of being afraid when you've got nothing to lose? When you're down and out? I felt no attachment to this life, and when I imagined something happening to it that very day—a violent car crash—I didn't care if I died.

•

In the evening, we stopped at a motel in Mazatlán, and Ed said, "Elena and I are renting a single room. You can pay for your own room, but we're not sharing."

Asking to sleep in the van felt awkward, so I said, "I'll move on."

Elena looked at me with a troubled gaze. "But it'll be dark soon."

"Suit yourself," Ed said. "Good luck."

•

I got lost trying to find a phone book and wandered the streets until I happened upon a library with space for my tent under its stairs. I pitched my tent, angry with myself for being too ashamed to ask if I could sleep in the van. I slipped into my sleeping bag with my knife in my hand.

Later, a noise woke me—a movement outside the tent. I held my breath to listen and heard feet shuffle on the concrete. I crawled out of my bag, slipped on my shoes, and grabbed my knife. I thought maybe it was a rat—or a dog. But then I heard two voices whispering. How could I defend myself from inside my tent? I'd be ambushed.

I squeezed my knife and waited—ready to stab and slash and kick and punch and claw my way out of my tent like a trapped animal. All of a sudden, I was afraid to die. I thought of my mother. Outside, the sound of a zipper. A woman's voice. Then moaning. I relaxed and fell asleep through the sounds of their sex.

•

In the morning, I found a phone booth. I sifted through the pages looking for Hernandez-Hernandez when an old, white hearse drove past me—with nobody following it. I remembered the hearse slowly driving my father's casket away, after we'd felt the hard coldness of his face in the coffin, and my mother, with her arms around my sister and me, crying out to my father and screaming goodbye. It was the most depressing sound I'd ever heard.

Now, I imagined it was my body in that white hearse, and that my mother would call for me—for her boy who'd died on the streets of Mexico. I felt terrible.

I found Ignacio's number in the phone book. Ignacio Hernandez-Hernandez. Then I closed the book and decided to go home. I'd been gone from Canada for four and a half months. Winter would surely blow over soon.

•

I walked the highway north, smelling the fog and the dewy sugar cane field that glistened in the bright sun, and I got excited by the thought of contacting the driveaway service in Toronto about driving a car back to Canada.

Suddenly, the red van drove by me and stopped on the shoulder.

Elena stuck her head out of the window. "Hey, stranger."

I ran to the van and hopped in. Ed said they'd be driving to Tucson that day, but I decided to go no farther than Nogales. From there, I would call about driving a car back from Arizona. It would be cheaper to wait for a car in Mexico.

CHAPTER NINETEEN

In Nogales, I walked along the green border wall—a patchwork of corrugated metal panels decorated with flowers and painted crucifixes. A Mexican man with sketchy eyes approached. He spoke English with a *chulo* accent. "Hey homie, you want some K?"

"K?"

"Ketamine—everybody's doin' it in New York these days."

I shook my head. "New York's not really my scene. I just need a place to crash."

"Try the Espe." He pointed across the street to a business with a faded, yellow wall. Someone had painted "Hotel Esperanza" on its glass door a long time ago.

•

The door opened to a tiny, green lobby. Behind the counter, a chubby young man watched a Mexican soap opera. When he saw me, he crammed a handful of potato chips into his mouth, wiped his hands on his pants, and spoke with a mouthful. "*Buenas tardes.*"

"Hola."

"*¿Buscas un cuarto?*"

I dropped my backpack to the floor and leaned on the counter, noticing a hallway that led to an open courtyard. "Here's the thing: I have no money. I'm driving a car back to Canada from Arizona soon, and I need a place to sleep. You mind if I pitch my tent in the courtyard for the night?"

"Umm... No one's ever... done that." His eyes bounced from his desk papers to his TV and back to me. "You'll be gone in the morning?"

"I promise." I shook his hand. "What's your name?"

"Castiel."

"I'm David. Thank you so much."

Castiel came out from behind his desk and locked the front door. I followed him to the courtyard—a large concrete slab with a washer, clotheslines, and potted plants and cacti in the corner.

"You can pitch your tent over there, by the plants." He pointed to an open room. "If you need to use the washroom, you can use the one in there."

•

At night, I woke in the freezing desert cold, sore from sleeping on the concrete. I ducked into the open room, where I found two wool blankets in a closet. I folded one blanket under my sleeping bag, laid the second one over my bag, and slept like a chick in a warm nest.

I woke to the hot sun against my tent. In the lobby, I found Castiel asleep in his chair. It was already 9 a.m.

He opened his eyes. "*Buenos días*. How'd you sleep?" He stood and turned on the TV.

"Great, thanks."

"So, what's your plan today, *güero?*"

"I have to find a place to camp."

He laughed. "If you need to, you can stay for a few nights."

I shook his hand again, as if he'd saved my life.

•

I emailed the car service, and they placed me on a waitlist for a car from Arizona. After that, I got high and strolled through the sombre streets of Nogales all day, and I wondered if the gloomy faces I saw were those of sweatshop workers or gang members. I couldn't wait to leave Nogales, where Mexican life looked too hard and nobody smiled.

At the hotel that evening, the floor shined, and the room smelled of bleach. Castiel sat alone again, eating chips and watching the same Mexican soap opera. He caught me staring at his bag of Takis.

"Want some?"

I reached into the bag and pulled out a handful. I sat in a chair and watched the soap opera with him.

"Where you been all day?" he asked.

"Walking around. Exploring."

"You must love adventure, huh?"

"I'm tired of it," I said. "I think adventure follows me."

He chuckled. "Why would adventure *follow* you?"

"Maybe I asked it to," I said. "Would you like to buy some weed?"

"What would I want to buy that for?"

"How about a mini-cassette recorder? I'd give you a fair price."

He shook his head. "I don't have any money."

A scruffy man entered the lobby. He wore cargo pants and a baseball cap. He took a long look at me while talking to Castiel about a room. "What is this *güero* doing here?" he asked.

Castiel chuckled. "He speaks Spanish, but he's from Canada... David hitchhiked from Costa Rica. He's cool."

The man gave me an impressed nod, and I nodded back. Then he said goodnight and headed to his room in the courtyard.

"Maybe I could sell him some weed," I said.

"Don't bother him," Castiel said. He poked his head down the hall and waited for the man to enter a room. He whispered, "He's a *coyote*. He takes people across the border, through the desert."

"That's amazing!" I shouted, unable to control my voice.

"Don't tell anyone. He'll kill me."

"Of course I won't tell anyone."

•

Before sleep, I was smoking a joint outside my tent when whispering men entered the courtyard. I peered over the tent. Three *campesino* men in ragged clothing and carrying plastic bags entered the *coyote*'s room. They closed the door and I tried to eavesdrop on their conversation, but couldn't understand. I thought of selling my passport to one of them.

•

The next two days were spent mostly in an internet café digesting Bella Chevalier's notes, which revealed to me that I knew what to write, but had no idea how. So, I emailed schools about creative writing programs. On the third day, I got an email from the driveaway service that said they had a car ready for me in Phoenix. I ran back to the hotel and found Castiel in the courtyard.

"Hey man, thanks for everything. A car's ready. I'm leaving," I said.

"Leaving? Why now?"

"Because I have to pick up the car."

"Don't leave yet."

"What?"

"Don't leave. You can stay." He looked away. "You can sleep here... in a room."

He had his back to me. I thought I heard a sniffle. Was he crying? He shoved towels in a washer and slammed it shut. Then he opened it again, reached for the soap, poured some into the lid, and dropped it to the ground. Green soap splattered onto his shoes. "*¡Chingao!*"

I backed away, packed my sleeping bag, and kept an eye on Castiel. His reaction made no sense to me. Was he lonely? I folded up the blankets from my tent and smuggled them back into the room. Then I quickly tore my tent down, rammed it into my bag, and threw the bag on my back.

Castiel wouldn't look at me when I approached him.

"I'm sorry, but I need to go find a place to pawn my camping gear in Phoenix. Do you want my bag of weed? Maybe you can sell it?" No response. I put my hand out to shake his hand.

He looked at me with misty eyes. "Just stay."

"Huh? I have to go. I'm picking up a Lexus in Phoenix."

"Forget the Lexus!" His crackling voice rattled me. "Stay. I need your help around here."

"My *help*?"

"Yes. Why won't you help me?" he asked, yanking a pile of wet sheets out of a washer and shoving them at me. "Help me!"

"I'm sorry, but I have to get going." I dumped the sheets on the washer. "Thanks for letting me crash and all, but I have to leave now. There's no time."

"No time. No time!" he shouted.

I offered my hand again, but he tossed a sheet over the clothesline, and it fell between us.

•

At the border crossing, they corralled us through doorways to form lineups inside the station. I merged into one lineup and was pushed ahead, like I was being sucked into America through a meat grinder. I read a sign on the wall about fines, prosecution, and seizure of property if caught transporting illegal goods. Then it hit me—I still had the bag of weed in my backpack.

"Next!" An agent stood at a counter. She waved at me impatiently. "Where you off to?"

"Canada. I'm picking up a car in Phoenix, to drive to Toronto."

While the woman checked my passport, two officers near the exit—a male and a female—eyeballed me, clearly talking about me.

The agent stamped my passport and let me through. As I walked toward the exit, I avoided looking at the two officers, but they moved in.

"Excuse me. Where are you from?" The female officer asked.

"Canada."

They cracked up.

"Damn," the male officer said.

"He owes me five bucks," she said. You look like a real trekker."

CHAPTER TWENTY

The sun chased me into the narrow shadows of a sweltering southern Phoenix neighbourhood. I sat for a while on the curb outside a 7-Eleven. I had just learned that my car back to Canada had been cancelled.

I pined for eye contact with everyone who came in and out of the store, but was too ashamed to ask for help. An old man came whistling across the parking lot. He looked to be in his sixties, scraggy and tanned, with a patchy white beard and a shredded trucker hat. He nodded to me as he entered the 7-Eleven, then he exited, chomping on beef jerky, and walked right up to me.

"She's a hot one. Ya travellin'?" His dusty desert voice could have narrated a cowboy movie.

"Yeah. Heading back to Canada from Costa Rica."

He held out his bag of jerky. I snagged a thick piece. "Thank you."

"The name's Labor-Hall Stan." He sat beside me and shook my hand with his weathered paw. "Yeah... I did a lot of movin' around in my day too—used to hop trains up and down the West Coast and down to Mexico all the time—every winter. Matter of fact, I rode to Costa Rica in the sixties. Much easier back then, ya know."

"I'm sure it was... Do you know of any places to camp around here?"

He scratched his beard. "Tough to find empty spaces in these parts, kid. But, let's see... Now, first of all, don't hang around the South Side. This used to be a great place to hide out, but not anymore."

"Why not?"

"It's a bad crowd, that's all. The cops won't harass you for camping anywhere in the West End, but that's because they got their hands full with too many people getting murdered out there, so... Let's see... Okay, now... the East End is *fucked*! I mean, do not go to the East End, kid."

A mint-green Ford Ranchero pulled up. A woman with a straw sun visor stepped out. Labor-Hall Stan stood and stepped toward the car.

"Afternoon, ma'am. That a '59?"

She blushed as she headed into the store. "Sure is. Ain't she a beauty?"

To me he muttered: "Friend of mine had one of these cars, kid, back in... jeez, must'a been '72... '73." He removed his hat, palmed his hair back, and inched up to the car like a man approaching a casket. I thought he might forget all about me and walk off into the desert, but the Ranchero owner snapped him out of his daze when she exited the store and walked back to her car. We watched as the woman tried to start the car, but the engine wouldn't go.

"You fellas mind giving me a push?" she asked.

"Not at all, ma'am," Labor-Hall Stan said.

"Thank you. Darn thing—must be too hot out here."

I got up and tossed my backpack up against the store. The woman's kind smile and sunny Southern accent got me dreaming she'd take me home with her and feed me fried chicken and peach pie.

We plopped our hands on the burning hood. "Dang, that's sizzling!" Labor-Hall Stan shouted. But we backed the car out of its parking spot, dropped our shoulders against the trunk, and forced the boat out of the lot and into the street. My sweat dripped onto the bumper. My legs burned. I thought I'd faint. And with my backpack out of sight, we just rolled farther and farther down the street. The woman turned the key over and over, but the engine refused. Labor-Hall Stan looked over. "If this boat don't fire soon, I'm gonna shit myself!"

She threw her hands in the air and steered to the curb. Labor-Hall Stan and I doubled over behind the car, winded and vanquished.

"Darn it. She's dead. Sorry, fellas. I'll call my husband. Here, take this." She offered Labor-Hall Stan a five-dollar bill she had fished from her white purse. "Split it between the two of you, would ya?"

"Alright, ma'am. Thank you." Labor-Hall Stan took the bill. "Good luck with the car."

"What an easy couple of bucks." Labor-Hall Stan said, trailing behind me, as I hurried back to the store for my bag. "Don't worry," he said. "I'll split this five in the store, kid."

It relieved me to hear him say that, just as it relieved me to see my bag still in front of the store. "Would you like to buy some weed from me?" I asked.

"No thanks, kid. That stuff makes me *reeeally* stupid, and I gotta work the gun show this weekend."

When Labor-Hall Stan came out, he handed me two dollars and fifty cents.

"What I suggest to you, my friend, is to head *way* out east. Go down McDowell here—you can take the 17 bus, and it'll take you to Scottsdale Road, which turns into Rural Road. And then you take the number 62, I think, which will take you down to Chandler. And from Chandler, head east again till it becomes Williamsfield."

I had forgotten everything he'd said already, but he kept talking and I kept hoping he'd invite me somewhere else. I would have followed him anywhere.

"Then you follow Williamsfield, till you hit Power Road—you'll have to walk south from there—and at the bottom of Power Road, you walk about fifteen minutes into the bush till ya reach the river. It's where people camp out."

"Thanks for the directions, and the two-fifty."

He shook my hand. "Take care, kid."

Labor-Hall Stan crossed the street, but he looked back to me and shouted, "Remember, don't hang around the South Side too long, kid—lot of Navajos around here."

"What does that mean?"

He didn't answer.

I bought beef jerky and water and walked north because there were small mountains in the distance and Labor-Hall Stan had turned me off of every direction but north.

•

The mountains were too far to reach that day. I surveyed the neighbourhoods for places to sleep as I walked all afternoon with a white T-shirt over my head to shield me from the relentless sun. My back ached. The tops of my feet burned. I'd worn a hole at the toe of my shoe, and little rocks kept finding their way through. From their windows, people watched the fool lug his backpack through the city in heat-stroke weather.

A black Ford pickup pulled over beside me, and the passenger, a muscular guy with slicked black hair, waved me over. I didn't trust his thin-lipped, greasy smile.

"You hungry, friend?"

I kept walking. "No. I ate."

"You need some money?"

I stopped and approached. "Yeah."

He held out a five-dollar bill.

I put the bill in my pocket. "Thanks."

"Good luck, man." The truck drove ahead. But after a minute, it stopped again. I slowed my pace, hoping it would move on, but I inevitably caught up to it.

"Hey, man. You want some food? We have leftovers from our picnic."

He reached into the back seat and rooted through a cooler. The driver, a woman in her late thirties with straight, black hair, stared at me through dark sunglasses.

"We have some chicken here, some rice... and water." The man handed me a container and a large plastic jug of cool water with lemon slices floating around inside.

"Thanks, man."

"You're welcome. Take care."

They drove away. I crammed the food in my backpack and took a giant gulp from the jug before I strapped it to the outside of my bag and moved on. Minutes later, I walked up to their truck again. I pretended not to see them this time.

He called out, "Hey, you want some *real* food?"

"No."

"You want a burger?"

"No, thanks."

He leaned out his window as the truck drove alongside me. "We're on our way to a drive-thru, either way. We don't mind. We'll pick up a burger for you. How about you meet us at the entrance to Washington Park? It's up the road." He pointed ahead. "We look like Al-Qaeda hanging around the streets like this. Meet us in, like, ten or fifteen minutes, alright? We'll get you a burger and some fries. And a Coke."

"Okay, thanks." I figured if they bought me a burger, the food they'd already given me would keep me going tomorrow.

He slipped his sunglasses on and smiled a toothless grin. "It's no bother. We love to help."

At Washington Park, I sat near the entrance and drank water under a shady oak tree. There were several pretty women out for a stroll, but none of them paid any attention to me. Of course not. I needed a haircut. A shave. A shower. Up high, a black kite circled like a vulture. It occurred to me: Why would the couple in the pickup be going to a drive-thru if they had just come from a picnic? I spat the water out and looked into the jug, studying and smelling the liquid, which smelled of lemons, but maybe something else... I had visions of being drugged and tied up and raped. Visions of serial killers, of the Gainesville Ripper.

Far from the entrance, I hid behind a thick tree and kept an eye out for the sketchy couple. Soon, their black pickup turned into the park. They stepped out. The guy held a small fast-food bag and a drink. They sat on a picnic table and looked around for me, waiting for me to nibble at their bait, waiting to take me home and slice me open.

After a while, they went off in search of another victim.

I wandered deeper into the park and stayed there all day. I ate and drank only a little of their food and water, afraid I'd ingest too much and drug myself, but what a day—I'd scored food and water, and made over seven bucks.

Close to sunset, I hopped a chain-link fence at one end of the park and into another park, where I pitched my tent under a tree.

At night, something hit my tent. I sprung up and fumbled around in the dark for my shoes. Then it hit the tent wall again. It was a sprinkler, going off intermittently on a timer.

•

"Hey!"

I opened the tent flaps in the morning. Some jerk in a yellow golf shirt pointed his shiny pitching wedge at me.

"It's illegal to camp here! This is a golf course!"

"Okay, I'm leaving." I fell back inside my tent and rolled up my sleeping bag.

"I'm serious. I'll call the cops!"

"I know, man. I'm packing up."

I put my shoes on and tossed my loaded backpack outside, then stepped out and tore down my tent.

His ball lay in the tall, dewy grass close to my tent, far from the green.

"Your ball's right there." I pointed.

"That's it. I'm calling the cops!" He stormed off.

Stuffing the tent in my bag, I screamed, "Go ahead, I'll be gone before you get to the phone, asshole!"

I plucked his yellow golf ball out of the grass and flung it over the fence.

•

Closer to the mountains, a man in cowboy boots approached me at an intersection. He had long blond hair and a beard. He floated over like an angel, then gestured for something to write on. He was deaf. I handed him my notepad and pen, and he scribbled in the saddest chicken scratch I'd ever seen: *Headed North Sedona*.

The man pointed north.

Was he going to Sedona, or asking me if I was heading there? I shrugged. Then he shrugged. And then we carried on walking our separate ways. But as I moved away from him, a certain emptiness took over. What was in Sedona? Had he invited me? Maybe I could wait there for a car. Maybe he had a place for me to stay. What was I thinking? Why did I walk away from him? We could have become best friends. I ran back to the intersection. He was gone. I called out, "Hello?" but remembered he was deaf.

•

At the base of the mountains—actually, only small hills—a whole subdivision of bungalows surrounded the hillside. I cut through the yard between two houses. On my way, I filled my jug from a backyard water hose, then hiked up the rocky slope. In a minute or two, I reached the summit and sat on my bag. The two neighbouring peaks had been lopped off, with winding driveways carved into their sides. One had a house frame built on it, and the other had a giant real-estate banner pegged to its slope. I thought of Sedona. Should

I walk there tomorrow? I drank half the jug of water and poured the rest over my head.

With the sun low to the west, I left my bag and hiked down to refill my bottle in the same yard. This time, a fat man sat in a rocking chair on the back porch, smoking a cigar. I approached him, and he stopped rocking.

"Stay out of my yard, buddy."

I stopped before I smiled politely and held up my water jug as if to say, "It's not what you think. I only need water."

The man rose to his feet. His face turned red and contorted. "Don't you dare come in my yard, buddy!"

"I only wanted to ask—"

He slammed his palms against his banister and shouted like an exasperated sheriff, "I'm armed, you bum!"

"You'd shoot me over water?"

"Are you stupid, idiot?" He went into his house.

I ran up the mountain.

•

A police cruiser pulled up the winding driveway on the next peak. The cop glared at me through his shades. I picked up my backpack and climbed down the hillside until I fell out of the cop's sight. I waited on the slope for a few minutes, next to a giant *S* written with white rocks, then I poked my head up to see the cop drive away.

I stayed hidden on the hillside till dark, when the city lit up like rivers of smoldering magma, and helicopters patrolled overhead. I hid under my sleeping bag when a chopper came closer, its searchlight licking the mountainside. The light pierced through the green fabric, blinding me before it flew away.

•

At sunrise, I smoked a joint and weaved through the quiet residential streets in search of water. A tiny church rested on a sandy corner lot. I ran up the stairs, ready to pound on the doors for pity, ready to repent. But then I noticed the boarded-up windows.

For an hour, I sat in the cool dirt in the church's shade, ruminating, lamenting, pining, and praying. I lit another joint. A dead pigeon lay twenty feet from me. I imagined the bird had flown into the church and broken its neck on its hunt for forgiveness. A single feather stood up straight from its wing. It fluttered in the wind, as if today was the day it would detach itself and soar. I gathered pebbles and tossed them at the pigeon, trying to free its feather. I started to feel that if I didn't free the feather, a serious thing would happen. I must have thrown fifty stones, hitting the bird many times with a hollow, dead thud, but the feather held on.

Suddenly I had trouble breathing—my mouth was stuck closed. The harder I tried to open it, the more I panicked. Then the right side of my face went numb, and I felt a strange pressure in my skull, which I had to free myself from by shaking my head.

I rose in a panic. My thoughts split into a hundred other thoughts, paranoid imaginings that raced toward the same conclusion: death. All I could think of doing was to run away, but when I tried to pull up my backpack, I dropped to the dirt, face-up. I closed my eyes and heard a throbbing against my eardrum, like my pulse was trying to squeeze a blood clot toward my brain.

My mind detached from my body. I felt as though I were floating, about to disconnect and drift into darkness forever.

"What happened to you?" a woman asked. She stood on the road, a bony woman out for a jog.

"I'm going to faint." The words came out in a slow, defeated whimper. My legs convulsed. Soon, it would take over my body. "Look at my legs."

"Are you sick?"

I shook my head. "Something's happening." I looked up at her as she stepped closer. I could only manage to whisper. "There's something wrong with my brain... It's happening. This is it. It's happening. Call an ambulance, please. It's a stroke. I can't move."

Then there were feet shuffling around me, and the woman said someone had run to find a paramedic who lived up the street.

"I need you to write down my email password," I said.

"What? Why?"

"I wrote a book. I emailed it to myself. I want my family to read it."

She pulled a pen and paper from her satchel. "Okay... ready."

"Under..."

"Under?"

"Under my sombrero."

"What?"

I managed to laugh. "The password is undermysombrero. All one word."

"Okay, got it."

A young Asian man rushed over.

"I'm a paramedic," he said. "What seems to be the problem?"

"I'm having a stroke," I said. "My legs feel like plastic."

He examined my eyes, then asked me to smile, lift my arms in the air, tell him my name, tell him where we were. I managed to follow his instructions.

"You're not having a stroke," he said.

"Yes, I am. Could you send my backpack to my nephew?"

"You'll be fine."

The woman carried my backpack, and the paramedic helped me walk to the front of the church, where he sat me on a bench. I closed my eyes and immediately floated in enclosed blackness with no sense of up or down, as if tethered within a womb. But outside the womb, the paramedic's voice carried on.

When I opened my eyes, the woman was gone, and a black man and his teenage son were sitting on the bench next to mine. The paramedic was checking for a pulse.

"I know this must seem strange," I said to the black man. "You sit next to this guy with a huge backpack, and he's rambling on to you about his mom..."

The man and his son stared straight ahead.

I'd said nothing to him about my mother.

"Oh my Lord, it's happening!" a woman shouted up the street.

"What's happening?" I whispered. Then I called out, "Is it manageable?"

No one acknowledged me. I heard quiet laughter, and it made me smile. "This city does need more laughter, don't you think?"

The paramedic looked at me, puzzled. For a moment, the black man's lips parted, as if he might speak important words to me, but he whispered to his son instead.

"I wish I could have finished my book before I died," I told them. "I hadn't slaved enough, you know? I could have written a book about Mac, too. Poor Mac. He just... went dark, like his light turned off. You ever known anyone like that?"

The black man cracked a small smile before he and his son got up and walked away.

"Dave, what's happening?" the paramedic asked. "Do you still think you had a stroke?"

"Oh...yeah." I'd forgotten about the stroke.

"Why would you think that?"

"It's just... I'm not here," I said. "I mean, my body is still here, but my consciousness seems to be...slipping out."

"Meaning?"

"I keep floating. When I close my eyes, I float away."

"Have you done any drugs?"

"I smoked a bit of weed. Why?"

"Because this can happen when you mess with street drugs."

"This isn't drugs. This is something else. I've done a lot of drugs—hard drugs. I'm not high. I'm just...slipping away."

"You never know with street drugs. Someone could have laced it... It sounds like drug-induced psychosis."

"What do you mean, like portals?"

"What? You have to be careful. Psychosis can be a precursor to schizophrenia... I saw your backpack... Are you going to the shelter?"

A homeless shelter. What a great idea. "Yes. Where is it, again?"

"Seventh and Seventh," he said.

"Seventh and Seventh?"

"Seventh Avenue and Seventh Street. The best thing for you is to go there and rest."

At a 7-Eleven, I bought a bottle of water. I couldn't count. I kept handing over coins until the guy behind the counter told me to stop. Outside, I pulled the bag of weed out of my backpack and tossed it in the trash.

CHAPTER TWENTY-ONE

At a small yellow gatehouse on a residential street flanked by empty sandlots, a gaunt, older man with a long white beard inched across the front porch, hunched over his cane.

"Is this the homeless shelter?" I asked.

Without taking his eyes off the ground, he pointed ahead with a long, crumpled finger and whispered, "Second door on the left." There was only one door.

When I walked past a tinted picture window, someone inside punched the glass and startled me. I opened the door to an office and found a tattoo-covered redhead seated in a chair by the window, with a big grin on his face.

"Gotcha good," he said. "Third one today."

Across from him, a lanky black man in a white tank top sat at a wooden desk. He looked about thirty years old and talked like he called the shots.

"Checkin' in?"

"I guess so."

"Are you committed to not using drugs or alcohol?"

"Sure. I don't have any on me."

"I'm serious. No drugs or alcohol while you're here."

"No problem."

He turned to the redhead and said, "Go find someone to check him in."

The redhead looked annoyed, but he got up and went outside. A giant in/out board hung on the wall. It listed thirty names—all men.

"My name is Charles," the black man said.

"David."

The door swung open. A grumpy-looking brute stood in the doorway. He had grey hair and wore an old denim jacket.

"This is Gary," Charles said. "He'll check you in."

With a stack of papers under his arm, Gary limped across the porch, then waved me over to a picnic table, where he dropped the papers. I sat across from him. He pulled a pen from his breast pocket. Faded green tattoos poked out from under his sleeves.

"We have to fill out your information... Name?"

"David."

He printed slowly, and said, "D.A.V.E."

"No. *David.*"

"It's the same name."

"How can they be the same, when they're different?"

He shook his head. "What's your drug of choice?"

"Huh?"

"Your favourite drug."

"Why?"

He held his pen over the empty field. "We have to."

"Marijuana?"

Watching Gary struggle to spell made me feel sober—like the tail end of an acid trip. And with the sensation of being grounded again came the sad realization that maybe there was something wrong with me—something wrong with my brain. Maybe all the fun had been had, and I could never get high again, or I'd lose my head for good next time.

"Okay. So, what's your second...secondary drug of choice?"

"What? Why?"

"They want to know."

I leaned in to glance at Gary's forms. The header read: *Transitional Living Communities - Narcotics Anonymous*.

"Is this not a homeless shelter?"

"Huh?"

"I think maybe I should go."

"Where?"

Good question. Where would I go? I could spend the night here, eat something, and start fresh in the morning.

"Never mind," I said. "I'll stay."

"Secondary drug?"

"I don't know...mushrooms?"

"How long since your last...since *you* last used *your*...first drug of choice?"

"Probably two hours."

Gary continued to read, "Breakfast time is from 5 a.m. to 6 a.m. Monday to Friday, and 6 a.m. to 7 a.m. on weekends..."

•

I followed Gary to three shacks built in a C-shape. Between the shacks lay a sandy courtyard bordered by rocks covered in flaking white paint. Gary opened the door to my unit, and we stepped into a dark room furnished with a pair of bunk beds, a floor lamp, and two nightstands. At the end of a narrow hallway was a small bedroom and washroom.

Gary pointed to one of the single beds in the bedroom. "This is yours." Then he left me standing in the hallway. "See ya later."

Someone had taped a sheet of paper over my bed and written *DAVE LEBRUN APRIL 1st* with a black marker. The name over the bed next to mine read *OLLIE OLLIE*. I regretted using my surname. I sat on the edge of the bed and waited for someone to tell me to leave, either because my purported drug addiction did not qualify me for treatment, or because a Canadian simply couldn't stay here. Maybe they'd stop me at the border and have me repay them.

The front door opened.

"Dave?"

I got startled, then stepped out of the bedroom.

Gary stood at the door. "You need to read these." He handed me some papers and pamphlets and turned away. "Meetin's at 6:30."

Ten-minute telephone privileges. House chores must be completed every day by 6:45 a.m. No headgear, sunglasses, eating, or smoking permitted under any roof. Do not walk on the grass or rocks. One one-hour "sleep-in" is allowed per week, and must be approved by management.

The pages detailed the functions of the "buddy" board, the "sign-out" board, and the "consequence" board. I came to the meeting schedule. House and Small Groups on Tuesdays and Thursdays from 6:30 to 8:30 p.m., Relapse Group on Sundays, and Big Book study on Wednesdays.

Today was Wednesday.

A bell rang outside. "Chow time!" someone shouted.

Men lumbered out of their units—pale, grubby characters who kicked dirt in the air as they moved toward a small window behind the gatehouse. I approached, not looking anyone in the eyes, and waited in line. A wiry young man served roast beef sandwiches. The men took their sandwiches to their units and ate on the stairs in groups. I did the same, alone, trying to blend into the scenery. The sandwich was too salty—more fat and bone than meat. I dumped most of it in the garbage and kept the lettuce, but then discovered a dead caterpillar in its folds.

I tossed the lettuce out, and a man who walked by asked with a hoarse voice, "What's the matter?" He was a brawny biker-type with long blond hair, and he wore pink, star-shaped plastic sunglasses.

"I don't eat caterpillar sandwiches," I said.

He looked at me as if I'd said the opposite, then walked on.

•

I took a cool shower. I stayed in there for a long time, scrubbing the dirt off me, lathering myself up with someone's lavender shampoo, drinking from the shower head, and cooling the back of my sunburned neck. Outside the washroom window, it was desert and the distant rusty mountains. In the window frame, a dead fly lay trapped in a cobweb.

I thought of running.

•

"Meetin' time!" a voice shouted from the courtyard, jolting me awake from a nap. I lay still, thinking they'd forget me, listening to the opening and closing doors and the grouchy voices of men lumbering out of their units. There must have been a hundred of them. I wasn't going anywhere. They would definitely forget about me, I thought. But then someone pounded on my door. "Meetin' time. Let's go, Dave!"

I joined a dozen men on their sluggish walk to a sandlot behind the units. Enclosed in chicken wire fencing, five rows of plastic chairs faced a folding table. The men filled the back rows first, and I wound up in the second row, terrified I'd have to speak about my made-up addiction.

Charles walked to the front and sat on the table. He wrapped his hands around the edge and swung his feet. "Everyone, remove your hats, beanies, and so on." He bowed his head. "God, grant me the serenity to accept the things I cannot change, the courage to change the things I can, and the wisdom to know the difference."

"Amen," the men said.

Charles stood up from the table. "My name is Charles, and my drug of choice is cocaine. I want the new guys as of Thursday to stand and introduce themselves and tell us what their drug of choice is."

I waited.

"Come on. Fucking new guys!" This got me out of my seat; two other men followed me.

"Alright. You first."

Charles had pointed at me, but a long-haired man behind me said, "Ken, methamphetamine."

"Lester, speed."

"Uhh, David... marijuana."

Several voices muttered things, and a younger, skinny guy who sat in front of me snorted. "That don't count."

"Thanks, guys," Charles said. We sat again. "I want to start by doing tag team. I'll tag someone and he has to get up and tell us why he's here, how he's feeling, and so on."

Charles scanned our chairs. His eyes quickly found mine. I looked away. Charles pointed to the older man from the porch who sat in my row. He stood with some difficulty. He had a large gash on his forehead now. "The name's Hector. My drug of choice is heroin... I'm not grateful for any of this. I have nothing else to say. Who do I tag?"

"Tag anyone."

The biker with pink, star-shaped sunglasses was tagged. He talked for ten minutes straight. "Keith, cocaine... I didn't get the job I applied for yesterday. But today's alright. I played frisbee with a kid at the park. He had a hot mom. Days like today are why I can never go back to jail." Keith patted the shoulder of a large Native American man who sat beside him. "If any of the new guys need some help, they can come to me and Randy here. We've been around, and we can help you adjust. We're the friends you haven't met yet."

Keith lowered his glasses, peered straight at me, and pointed.

I stood. "My name is David, and I guess I'm here—"

"What's your drug of choice?" someone asked.

I mumbled, "Marijuana."

"Speak up," someone said.

"I don't know what to say," I said. "Maybe being here, listening to you guys, you know...maybe I'll learn something."

The skinny guy in front of me laughed. "Yeah, they're a bright bunch of guys!"

I laughed too, but quickly stopped myself. None of the dull faces around us were laughing. "I've been hitchhiking across Central America and Mexico for five months... I guess I'm here because I've got three dollars left and I had nowhere else to go."

The skinny guy slung his arm over his chair.

"You run away from problems?" he asked.

"Maybe."

The skinny guy faced Charles. "I been readin' that book you gave me, about escapes—how that's good therapy for a time—being in a new place, or having a new girl or a new drug makin' us happy all over again." He turned back to me and looked me straight in the eyes. "But if we don't look inside and change, the new gets old pretty damn quick. And then we're off again, looking for anything new, just to get away from the old."

"Thank you," Charles said. "What do you think about that, David?"

"Yeah, I've left a lot of places—a lot of people."

"People who needed you?" Charles asked.

I tried to speak, but got choked up and tried to hide it by closing my eyes and nodding.

"Good work," Charles said. "Tag someone else."

I tagged the skinny guy, and he stood and told his story. One by one, the men then tagged each other to speak, to see if they could find something buried inside.

"Meeting over?" someone shouted.

"No—two minutes left," Charles said.

"Thirty seconds by my watch," another voice protested.

Charles hopped off the table and shouted, "We use my watch! Now, guys, I know we all signed the ninety-day commitment."

What? *Ninety* days?

"Now, I know it's a voluntary shelter, but I want to commit again to you now. I want to commit to my forty days left." Some of the men agreed, with feeble applause.

Half the men walked away, and the other half walked to Charles. I thought I'd look suspicious if I left too soon like I planned to run off, so I approached Charles' group. We formed a circle and wrapped our arms around each other's necks. "Put your right foot forward," Charles said. We all put our right foot forward. Charles began to pray again, and the men repeated each line. "Lord, help me use this day for good and not for ill. Make time a gift, not something to kill. Help me crowd this day with fleeting chances, to aid a needy brother, to open wide my heart."

"Amen," they said.

As I opened the door to my unit, Charles shouted, "Now, I've caught guys sneaking out before. I want y'all to know I'm up every night till 4 a.m., alright? If you try to leave, I'm gonna catch you."

•

My unit stayed empty for the rest of the evening. I thought of not turning my back on these men. But I needed to go home—to commit ninety days to my family.

I showered again, propped my backpack by the door for quick access, placed some clothes on the foot of the bed, and set my shoes under the bed. It was only 8 p.m. I could fall asleep now, wake up at 4 or 5 a.m., and walk away. I lay down and went to sleep.

When I woke up I turned over in bed. Ollie Ollie, a large black man, was in his bed with his back to me. Light bled through the crack in the curtain.

Without a sound, I got dressed, threw my bag on my back, and crept out of the bedroom. In the front room, four men slept on the bunk beds. I recognized Hector from the gash on his forehead.

As I opened the door, I bumped the floor lamp with my bag. It fell over like a chopped tree, but I caught it before it hit the floor.

Easing myself out of the unit, I realized the sky was still black. I'd mistaken the streetlight for sunrise. Inside the room, the alarm clock read: 2:53 a.m.

I gently closed the door and scanned the units as I snuck across the courtyard, expecting to find Charles watching me. But no one appeared in the small windows. I heard faint voices as I neared the gatehouse. As I walked alongside the gatehouse, the voices grew louder—the voices of two men on the front porch.

When I stepped out from beside the gatehouse, I walked fast toward the sidewalk. Keith and Randy sat at the picnic table, smoking.

Keith stood and said, "Can I help you?"

I kept walking and only turned to them once I made it to the sidewalk.

"Hey, were you with us yesterday?"

"Yeah, but—"

"You're leaving already?"

Their steady gaze worried me. I thought they might come after me, so I walked faster.

"I'm alright, guys. I just needed a place to crash. I'm going to see my mom."

Keith nodded, and they went back to talking.

I walked down the sidewalk. A man with shaggy blond hair approached. For a second, I thought the deaf man had come back and would lead me to Sedona. But as we passed each other, he slowed down, stole a look at my backpack, and drawled, "Go-in' to Ca-li-fooor-nia?"

"Nnnnnnope."

CHAPTER TWENTY-TWO

I had hidden behind a Baptist church until sunrise, and thought of looking for work at a motel or bed-and-breakfast, where they could put me up until a car from the driveaway service was ready. A phone book search led me to a bed-and-breakfast not too far away, in a brick mansion on a half-acre lot.

A "for sale" sign was staked in the middle of the yard. A Hispanic man stood atop a ladder with a long pole. He was picking oranges from a tree.

"Excuse me," I said as I walked up the driveway.

"Oh, Jesus Christ! You scared me." The man stepped down the ladder. He had a trimmed moustache and spoke with an effeminate lisp.

I gave him the story in Spanish. "Could I work here for food and a place to pitch my tent?"

The man smiled. "I'm Hugo. Let's ask Dan. He's the boss." He carried his basket of oranges into the house.

Moments later, another man came out. He had a white beard and a beer belly. His voice was kind—the voice of a man accustomed to hosting strangers. He took a close look at my backpack. "You really hitchhiked all this way from Costa Rica?"

"Mostly."

An approving nod. "The bed-and-breakfast is closed down, but you're welcome to pitch your tent in the yard."

We walked to a shaded area by the porch. I dropped my bag and pulled out my tent. "Thank you so much. It'll be nice to leave my stuff somewhere. I need to find work while I wait for the car."

"How long ya been on the road?"

I looked up while I pitched my tent. "About five months, I think... You know of any places I can work for cash around here? Construction or landscaping, maybe?"

"Have you ever painted houses?"

"Yeah."

"If you want, you can do some painting here."

"Sounds great to me."

"I can pay...let's see, how about four hundred to paint the kitchen, upstairs hallway, and two bedrooms?"

I stood and shook his hand, but I wanted to hug the guy.

We had breakfast on the porch: eggs and toast with avocado and salsa, oranges, and fresh coffee. I delighted Hugo with my Spanish and entertained them with stories of my five-month adventure, from which they'd so mercifully rescued me.

After breakfast, I cannonballed into the deep end of the pool and sank to the cold bottom, where I screamed for joy. I dragged myself onto a large inflatable turtle, lay on my back, and closed my eyes. I remembered our old family home—afternoons in our backyard swimming pool with my little sister—the house lost forever with my father gone and mother now in a small apartment in a complex for the disabled. Tears streamed down my face and into the pool.

CHAPTER TWENTY-THREE

The car owner was an elderly lady from East York. After I loaded her boxes in the trunk of the new BMW, I took off in the early afternoon.

When I hit Route 87, I felt a rush of freedom, safety, and comfort, and when I reached Tonto National Forest—the city far behind—I rolled down the window and let out a shrill like a triumphant lunatic.

I stopped for gas and fast food in West Mesa, Albuquerque, and then drove on and on in a haze through the barren landscapes of the Great Plains, until I arrived in Amarillo, Texas around 1 a.m. I drove around looking for a cheap hotel and couldn't find one, but I was too wound up to sleep anyway, so I left Texas and zipped past Oklahoma City, all alone on I-44, and finally pulled over at a rest area outside Tulsa in the middle of the night.

I woke at 4 a.m. and couldn't go back to sleep. So I fuelled up, ate a muffin, and carried on, listening to a book on tape that I'd found in the glove compartment—Mordecai Richler's *Barney's Version*: "...bad night, couldn't sleep since I was in for one of those old fart's nights, rewinding the spool of my wasted life, wondering how I got from there to here..." And here I was, only twenty-five and already in for so many of those awful nights—tormented by mistakes.

But no more.

•

I arrived at the Canadian border in Detroit, red-eyed and drunk-looking, but they let me through. I pulled over to exchange my remaining two hundred U.S. dollars, shivering in my wool sweater and shorts.

After dropping off the car, I rode the subway to the Greyhound station. Waiting for the bus outside, I made a collect call to my mother. And after telling her I was back in Canada, I said, "Mom, I feel bad for leaving after you had your stroke."

"That's okay. You don't have to feel bad about that."

"Yes, I do. And I also wish we'd talked about Dad's death."

Her silence was expected. She couldn't speak of these things—nobody had taught her.

"I guess we were all too scared," I said.

She said something, but the bus had pulled up, and her voice was difficult to hear—like I was being pulled away, and the phone cord had stretched to a fine filament—and I kept saying, "Mom, I'm coming home."

At dawn, I woke up on the bus. We had stopped. And because everyone on the bus was talking—unlike in Latin America, Canadians never talk to one another on public transit—I knew there'd been an accident. Up ahead, on the icy, narrow highway, was a long row of brake lights and car exhaust. We had just crossed the bridge where my friend and his parents had died so many years ago. Surrounded by the snow-covered spruce forests and darkness, I peered outside my frosted window when we reached the ambulance, police, and tow-truck lights. A pickup truck had turned over. A car's front end was wrecked. The truck driver was speaking with police. A man and his wife sat on the ambulance bumper, and two young boys sat on a gurney, wrapped in blankets. Everyone was okay, and we left the wreck behind us.

CHAPTER TWENTY-FOUR

In Timmins, I walked in my shorts across the crunchy snow, the crisp whiteness of winter pinching my skin. The tree branches were exposed like skeletons. It smelled like Christmas and street hockey. I hopped into a warm cab.

The lights were out in my mother's apartment. Her bedroom door was closed. I turned on the electric fireplace and lay on the warm sofa that smelled like jasmine candles. Still stuck to the refrigerator was a magnet that belonged to my father. It read: *Dave's Things To Do*. I pulled seventeen notepads from my bag and stacked them in order—a tower sculpted out of all the dirt I'd dragged myself through. Admiring my tower, I thought of the car owner in Florida, asking me why I'd want to write about "dirt" like Juan-Carlos assaulting a woman, and then I knew why—why I wanted to write about the dirt, about rage, dread, and dejection, about exhaustion and shame—because these were things to heave and excrete, to scrub off, and to shape into art— something to put on a shelf and forget about.

•

I had fallen asleep to the purr of the fish tank filter and the ticking of the kitchen clock, like the beating of a heart.

I woke to the sound of my mother's creaky rocking chair and the news on TV.

While I pretended to sleep, I felt it when she looked at me—my long hair, dirty clothes, sunken face. She phoned my sister and whispered when my nephew answered, "Good morning, it's your *memère*... Can you tell your mom your uncle is home?"

I opened my eyes and knew I'd stay here as long as it took for us to learn to do things like hug and say "I love you," and to feel like a family again.

My mother leaned forward and said, "Welcome home." Then she hobbled over to the kitchen with her dead arm in its brace. "You want a coffee?"

"Okay." I wiped a tear from my face. "Mom, how old would my older sibling have been, if you hadn't had a miscarriage?"

"They would have been born between you and your sister."

I sat up. "Didn't that happen *before* me?"

"No," she said. "You were my first. You're the big brother."

I thought: all this time believing I wasn't meant to be an older brother...

Above the living room window hung a wooden carving my father bought for my mother twenty-five years earlier. I read it—the words my mother taught us to read: *Grow old along with me, the best is yet to be.*

On the TV was a story about the hundreds who jumped out of burning towers on 9/11. The footage of them pushed out of their windows by fire, and falling together, made me think of my father. Suddenly, I understood why he never said goodbye.

Maybe it wasn't cancer that killed my dad. Maybe it was learning he would have to leave us that killed him. Maybe it killed so much, he couldn't even say goodbye.

I could live with that.

EPILOGUE

Twenty-two years later, I am again on my mother's couch while she sits in her La-Z-Boy. There are leftover 70th birthday balloons on the walls. There is an oxygen tube up her nose, hypodermoclysis running to her gut, and two open IV ports in her bandaged arms.

In half an hour, the doctor and nurse will arrive with the drugs to first put her to sleep, then put her in a coma, then numb her veins, then stop her breathing, and then stop her heart. But we have no regrets. While she battled her cancer, my sister and I spent half of the last eight months with her, facing death and saying goodbye. Because after twenty years of tumult and self-destruction, I finally developed a good relationship with my family—one that eventually came at the expense of my friendship with people like Mac, who never outran the shadowy figures, who two months after my mother's death, and ten years after my attempted intervention, would be found dead in his Toronto apartment.

•

The doctor and nurse have my mother propped up on a wedge cushion in bed so she can look at us, but she has to move up higher. I put my arms under her, pick up her ninety-pound body and lay her down—but I mostly just wanted to pick her up. I start crying as I hold her head and kiss her and say, "I'm going to miss you." And she cries.

My sister sits on my mother's right side, by her head—my brother-in-law next to my sister. My nephew is next to him. Kate, my partner, sits at my mother's feet. And I sit on the edge of the bed, beside my mother, holding her left hand because the right one has been dead for twenty-seven years.

What do you say now? This moment of death. You can only comfort and try to assure them everything is going to be okay for you and for them, but you have no idea. You have no idea what will happen to her when she's gone. Maybe she's going to see your father and her parents and her little brother, or my unborn sibling. Or maybe, it's just lights out and she and they never exist again. But that's not comforting. So, we tell her again that she's going to float out of her body, and when she does, she should just go. "Don't haunt us," I say.

My mother sighs. She's tired of this talk. She's tired of this prolonged goodbye.

We think of other things to say, like, "You made it, mom. You lasted eight months and made it to your 70th birthday. We're proud of you. And we're all here and we love you."

The doctor asks if she's ready and my mom enthusiastically says, "Let's do this!" before she and my nephew share a loud high-five. Then the doctor inserts the first syringe into the IV port.

I watch the doctor's thumb slowly press down on the syringe. I know she'll slip into sleep now. I say, "Mom, you don't have to say anything else. You can let go. We know you love us. You've said it all." I say that because I don't want her to mumble something, and have that incoherent goodbye haunt us for the rest of our lives.

But, as her breathing slows and her eyes look heavy, she says, "I love you all." And she looks at my sister and says her name. She looks at my brother-in-law and says his name. Then there's a pause. The drug is hitting her—she looks dazed. And then I think, she'll never get to us all. But she looks at my nephew and says his name. I see her falling asleep, but trying to keep her eyes open. And it begins to feel like she's going away, and struggling to remember our names—wanting to look at us and say our names as a way to remember—to take a memory of us with her. She looks at Kate with droopy eyes and says her name. Then she looks at me, but her eyes close.

I quickly accept that mine is the only name she won't get to say. It doesn't matter to me, but I wanted this moment to be perfect for her. I just wanted her to leave with dignity.

Her eyes open and she says, "David."

And we all have a hand on her now, and everything is tender as we say we love her over and over, until her eyes close for the last time.

And as I hold and rub her hand, and see the veins into which the doctor dumps one syringe after the next, I realize how old her skin looks, and pounding in my chest now is the helpless feeling that her life happened too fast. And I just want it to slow down, to say I love you and goodbye once more, to hold on a little longer, before it stops.

THANK YOU

To all the beta readers, consultants, and editors (in order of appearance):

Emma Darwin, Leslie Ferguson, Jessica Jo Hoover, Eva Smith, Glenn Orgias, Tennessee Jones, Janet Steen, Joshua Mohr, Samantha Lord, Carolyn Dekker, Diane Young, Joe Walters, Jeff Petersen, Jake Glass, John Lake, Stacy Lundeen, Oliver Rivas, John Julius Reel, Nick Gardner, Alexander Smith, Jaylynn Korrell, and Gerald Brennan at Tortoise Books.

To my family, Suzy, Noam, Jesse, for always being there.

To my love, Sharlene, for your proofreading, editing, patience, and support.

To my mother, Marie-Paule, for reading the manuscript in her final days and offering the best feedback of them all: "I'm just happy he came home."

ABOUT THE AUTHOR

David LeBrun is a multi-lingual French-Canadian author. With a gritty and minimalist style, his writing draws from his travels and offbeat perspectives. His short stories have appeared in *Blank Spaces Magazine* and *Caesura*. *Delirium Vitae* is his first of three memoirs. He lives in Montréal, Québec, where he plays hockey, consults on screenplays, and works as a technician in the art department of the film industry.

ABOUT TORTOISE BOOKS

Slow and steady wins in the end, even in publishing. Tortoise Books is dedicated to finding and promoting quality authors who haven't yet found a niche in the marketplace—writers producing memorable and engaging works that will stand the test of time.

Learn more at www.tortoisebooks.com or follow us on Bluesky @tortoisebooks.bsky.social.

www.ingramcontent.com/pod-product-compliance
Lightning Source LLC
Chambersburg PA
CBHW032224080426
42735CB00008B/699

YOUR FREE GIFT
with this bundle is double!

Thank you for purchasing this book.
Click on this link to download these FREE tools!!!

http://bit.ly/chidlrencommunicationtips

http://bit.ly/becomingadad

Note: If you have purchased the paperback format then you need to write this link on your browser search bar. These tools are useful resources to:
1. Understand the development of the language and communication of children. It is also a checklist for language and listening skills that will provide you with effective tips.
2. Hospital bag checklist for dads (also for moms and your newborn baby!). A quick reference list of important things you'll need to pack for birth, when the baby arrives you'll want to have the right stuff on-hand!

Table of contents

BECOMING A DAD

The First-Time Dad's Guide to Pregnancy Preparation(101 Tips for Expectant Dads)

INTRODUCTION 1

CHAPTER 1: HOW DO YOU KNOW SHE IS PREGNANT? 3

CHAPTER 2: GETTING READY TO BE PARENTS 16

CHAPTER 3: TALKING ABOUT THE FUTURE 23

CHAPTER 4: EARLY PREPARATIONS 35

CHAPTER 5: FINANCES 45

CHAPTER 6: PREPARING YOUR HOME 60